THE BRITISH IMPERIAL CENTURY, 1815–1914

Critical Issues in History

The British Imperial Century, 1815–1914: A World History Perspective
by Timothy H. Parsons

THE BRITISH IMPERIAL CENTURY, 1815–1914

A World History Perspective

TIMOTHY PARSONS

ROWMAN & LITTLEFIELD PUBLISHERS, INC.
Lanham • Boulder • New York • Toronto • Oxford

ROWMAN & LITTLEFIELD PUBLISHERS, INC.

Published in the United States of America
by Rowman & Littlefield Publishers, Inc.
A wholly owned subsidary of The Rowman & Littlefield Publishing Group, Inc.
4501 Forbes Boulevard, Suite 200, Lanham, Maryland 20706
www.rowmanlittlefield.com

PO Box 317
Oxford
OX2 9RU, UK

British Library Cataloguing in Publication Information Available

Library of Congress Cataloging-in-Publication Data

Parsons, Timothy, 1962–
    The British imperial century, 1815–1914 : a world history
perspective / Timothy Parsons.
        p.   cm. — (Critical issues in history)
    Includes bibliographical references and index.
    ISBN 0-8476-8824-0 (cloth : alk. paper). — ISBN 0-8476-8825-9
(pbk. : alk. paper)
        1. Great Britain—Colonies—History—19th century.   2. Great
Britain—Foreign relations—19th century.   3. Great Britain–
–Colonies—History—20th century.   4. Imperialism—History—19th
century.   5. Imperialism—History—20th century.   6. World
politics—19th century.   I. Title.   II. Series.
DA16.P3176   1999
941.08—dc21   99-11765
                                                                                                    CIP

Printed in the United States of America

CONTENTS

MAPS

FOREWORD

Set to serve the lands they rule,
(Save he serve no man may rule),
Serve and love the lands they rule;
Seeking praise nor guerdon
                    —"A School Song"

R udyard Kipling's incantation, found at the beginning of *Stalky and Co.,* captures the sense of service, indeed mission, that provided much of the rationale for British imperialism in the nineteenth century. Although Kipling can be read too easily as an apologist for empire, he conveys the pride of the English colonial enterprise. Ideals of commerce, Christianity, and governance combined to justify the subjugation of indigenous people throughout Asia and Africa. Yet in the process of empire building, the dominant British culture would be informed and adjusted to native culture. For example, Kipling, especially in his early works, reveals the vast complexity of India with its agglomeration of racial and religious groups. The power of Indian culture affected Kipling's perception of the world, as it did English colonial culture in general. While English men and women maintained, perhaps with too much self-assurance, that they had a knack for ruling, many came to believe that "one race was not superior to another; the East had in some ways a better religion than the West; Gunga Din was a better man than the average Tommy; the Sudanese Fuzzy-Wuzzy and the Zulu were worthy of admiration as fighting men."

In the process of governing, the English created, as Timothy Parsons tells us, "a medium of cultural exchange which mixed and diffused the various cultures of the Empire around the globe." By placing the emergence of the British empire in the nineteenth century within a cultural context of world history, Parsons provides readers with a terse descriptive history of imperial acquisition, but more importantly he examines the political, social, cultural, and environmental consequences of the interaction of western and non-western peoples. Prior to the nineteenth century, the Imperial Century, Britain established colonies in North America and the Caribbean, as well as in India, the Cape Colony in southern Africa, and the New South Wales territory in Australia, plus various naval bases throughout the world. This empire expanded dramatically in the next century as Britain extended its reach throughout Asia and Africa. This empire grew out of competition with other European powers including France, Russia, Germany, and Italy. In China, the Japanese entered into this rivalry.

Yet, as Parsons informs us, the British acquired more territory and influence than any of its rivals. While some opposition to this empire arose at home among leading politicians who considered it an unnecessary expense, Britain continued to extend its empire throughout the first half of the nineteenth century. Beginning with the occupation of Egypt in 1882, Britain joined other European powers in the partition of Africa. In this same period, Britain gained formal control over Malaya, Upper Burma, and a number of islands in the South Pacific. As the Ottoman and Chinese empires weakened, Britain became embroiled in the internal affairs of these countries as well.

The purpose of the Critical Issues in History series is to provide readers with a short narrative and interpretative history of major events and movements in world history, based on the latest scholarship. Parsons fulfills the promise of this series by providing a concise and readable history of the emergence of the British empire in the nineteenth century. In doing so, he challenges his readers to question conventional assumptions about the global influence of British imperialism by showing how British and indigenous cultures influenced one another. While noting the transforming and far-reaching affects of British colonialism, he carefully balances this account by showing how Britain's subject populations often retained many of their pre-colonial institutions and traditions while adapting British imperial culture to suit local circumstances. Similarly, this empire introduced the British public to new words, languages, products, and values. The result was the emergence of a hybrid imperial culture at home and abroad.

Readers will find this fascinating and dynamic encounter between the West and the non-West especially appropriate in understanding our own world in the twenty-first century.

Donald T. Critchlow
Series Editor

1

INTRODUCTION

S uppose you are embarking on a tour of the world. Of the hundreds
of languages spoken today, you stand the best chance of making
yourself understood in most countries if you speak English. Although
the widespread use of English is partly due to contemporary U.S. cultural dominance, it is also a legacy of the global empire that Britain created during what Ronald Hyam has termed the "imperial century."
From the end of the Napoleonic Wars and the Congress of Vienna in
1815 to the beginning of the First World War in 1914, British imperialists spread their political, economic, and cultural institutions to the far-
thest reaches of the world. In addition to the global prevalence of English, this process also explains the widespread use of the parliamentary
system, the standard of driving on the left side of the road, the use of
bagpipes in national armies, and even the popularity of tea time.

Past historians tended to view this process as the "modernization"
of Africa and Asia through the introduction of Western culture and technology. In reality, British imperialism created a medium of cultural exchange that mixed and diffused the various cultures of the empire around
the globe. To be sure, Britain itself was the dominant political force during the imperial century, but British imperialists could govern their non-
Western subjects only by co-opting and adapting their social institutions.
This process produced an imperial culture that was never entirely British. Thus, although many Africans and Asians may drink tea when most
Britons drink it, they often prepare it in the Indian style by boiling the
tea along with milk, sugar, and spices. Similarly, this book is more than
just the story of how Britain acquired a global empire; it is an examination of the political, economic, social, and even biological consequences

1

of the interaction of Western and non-Western peoples over the course of the imperial century.

IMPERIALISM AND WORLD HISTORY

An empire is most often defined as a political unit that controls an extensive amount of territory and a heterogeneous mix of subject peoples. Territories located overseas are often known as colonies, especially if they were settled by migrants from the dominant group in an empire. The word "colony" comes from the Latin *colonia,* which referred to a Roman settlement in a conquered territory. The term was applied to the initial European conquest and settlement of North America and Australia, where most of the original inhabitants died out as a result of conquest, abuse, and disease. European expansion into the tropical regions of Africa and Asia in the nineteenth century, on the other hand, produced few actual colonies. These areas were unattractive to European settlers, and it was difficult (if not impossible) to stretch European political institutions to incorporate their largely unwilling African and Asian populations. The term "colony" also does not describe the informal influence of European powers in non-Western states that retained most of their sovereignty.

The word "imperialism" was first used in the mid-nineteenth century to describe the process by which a state either acquired formal jurisdiction over another people or gained substantial informal influence over their political, economic, and social affairs. The main difference between formal and informal imperialism was the degree of sovereignty surrendered by a subject population. Although this definition is relatively straightforward, the factors that led Britain and its rivals to adopt imperialistic policies in the nineteenth century have been the subject of considerable debate among historians. The most popular explanations have linked imperialism to the rise of militaristic nationalism, intense economic competition, and the linkage of new areas to the capitalist economies of Europe.

The common factor in these older causative debates is that they define imperialism as a largely European phenomenon. To be sure, Westerners were the instigators of the imperial enterprise, but defining imperialism solely as the extension of European influence fails to consider its impact on the peoples that it subjugated. Nineteenth-century imperialism can be alternatively defined as the global expansion of the industrial economy and culture of Europe, resulting in Europe's discovering and exploiting the tropical world. These new world empires broke down physical and political barriers by linking disparate regions under a unitary political or economic system. Therefore imperialism served as a medium of cross-cultural contact that diffused people, wealth, technology, and culture between the imperial European heartland, known as the metropole, and the subject African and Asian periphery.

Of course, it is also possible to interact through long-distance trade and international relations. Nineteenth-century imperialism, however, was produced by an often violent loss of sovereignty, which allowed the European powers to dictate the nature of these exchanges to serve their own interests at the expense of subordinate populations. Nevertheless, the imperial interface worked both ways, and Africans and Asians, in turn, had a degree of influence on the domestic institutions and cultures of imperial nations. Whereas the older empires of the eighteenth century sent large numbers of Europeans primarily to temperate regions in the Americas, the nineteenth century's multiethnic global empires produced a hybrid imperial culture through the greater interaction of diverse peoples and ideas.

BRITAIN'S IMPERIAL CENTURY

During the imperial century Great Britain added approximately 10 million square miles of territory and roughly 400 million people to its overseas empire. Although these figures include British settlements in Australia, Asia, and North America, most of the new holdings were in the tropical regions of Africa and Asia. In addition to these formal acquisitions, the British also obtained extensive informal influence in the new nation-states of South America and the much older Chinese and Ottoman Empires.

Britain was not the only European power to expand its imperial influence during this period. By the end of the nineteenth century its rivals included France, Russia, Germany, Italy, and, in the case of Asia, an expectedly powerful Japan. Nevertheless, the study of British imperialism provides the best insight into the nature of this global phenomenon because Britain was the pioneering imperial power and, as such, acquired more territory and influence than any of its rivals.

The British Empire certainly seemed to be in decline at the beginning of the imperial century. The thirteen American colonies had already been lost to revolution, and Britain's abolition of the slave trade in 1807 decreased the value of its sugar-producing colonies in the West Indies. India appeared to be the only exception to this trend as the British East India Company continued to consolidate its hold over the subcontinent. In 1815, the overseas British Empire consisted of the remaining North American colonies (which would eventually become Canada), India, the Cape Colony in southern Africa, the New South Wales territory in Australia, and a handful of naval bases scattered throughout the globe.

The territories in North America and Australia were primarily vestiges of the "old" imperialism, which had sent large numbers of Britons to settle regions with temperate climates approximating western Europe. Earlier histories of the British Empire have portrayed these areas as empty or underpopulated, but in reality the creation of settlement colonies invariably required the subjugation of non-Western populations. Unlike most of the Africans and Asians that Britain eventually encountered during the course of the imperial century, these aboriginal peoples were in a particularly vulnerable position because of their isolation and their limited political development. Australian Aborigines still relied on stone tools and had no governing institutions beyond loosely structured clans. As a result, the Aborigines and the Amerindian populations of the New World were virtually exterminated by epidemic disease and warfare in the first wave of European overseas migration in the seventeenth and eighteenth centuries.

Thus the continuing development of Britain's remaining settlement colonies in North America and Australia was not part of the process of informal empire and the "new" imperialism that governed British relations with Africa and Asia during the nineteenth century. The original inhabitants of these territories were reduced to tiny minorities as successive waves of settlers transplanted British culture and institutions to the New World. These settlement colonies followed a separate path of development during the imperial century as British imperialists gradually extended the privilege of self-government to their overseas "kith and kin."

As for Britain's remaining holdings in Africa, Asia, and the Caribbean, by midcentury British leaders had become so confident in the prosperity generated by their industrial strength and commitment to free trade that some influential politicians suggested that colonies were an unnecessary expense. Yet even during this period of official indifference to imperialism, the British continued to acquire useful territories. These included strategic and economic outposts in Singapore (1818), the Falkland Islands (1833), Aden (1839), Hong Kong (1842), and Lagos (1861). Britain also annexed new settler colonies in New Zealand (1830s) and Natal (1842), which were to follow trajectories that differed substantially from its territories in Australia and Canada. For the most part, however, midcentury imperialists preferred informal influence to formal rule.

Few in Britain foresaw that their empire would expand so rapidly and suddenly in the latter part of the nineteenth century. Beginning with the occupation of Egypt in 1882, Britain found itself with a new African empire through its partition of the continent among its European rivals. In Asia, the British acquired formal control over Malaya, Baluchistan, Upper Burma, and a host of islands in the South Pacific. In addition to these formal annexations, Britain also became more deeply enmeshed in the internal affairs of the Ottoman and Chinese Empires as these great Asian powers struggled to cope with Europe's new industrial might. Thus, instead of divesting themselves of their supposedly unnecessary overseas colonies, the British found themselves in possession of a truly global empire on the eve of the First World War. Although the ruling culture of the empire was British, it was, in fact, a hybrid institution encompassing a vast array of peoples, languages, and customs.

NEW INTERPRETATIONS OF EMPIRE

Almost as soon as the British Empire was established, historians struggled to explain the apparent ease and rapidity with which Britain acquired such an extensive empire. Britain's imperial subjects played little role in these debates, and, for the most part, historians have tried to explain what motivated Britain to acquire a new overseas empire in the nineteenth century. Some have argued that the scramble for territory in Africa and Asia after the 1880s was inspired by a "new imperialism" that represented a substantial break with Britain's imperial policies earlier in the century. Others, however, have countered that British policy remained largely constant throughout the imperial century and that it was increased political and economic competition from its European rivals that forced Britain to establish formal control over regions in which it previously had relied on informal influence to protect its interests.

In spite of these sharp disagreements over Britain's imperial motives, most historians have tended to assume that the ability to acquire an empire was a foregone conclusion because of British economic and military superiority. By most accounts, the demands it faced as the world's first industrial nation drove Britain to seek new sources of raw materials, new markets, and new areas for investment. This same industrial might provided Britain with the modern weapons, medicines, transportation systems, and communications that made it easy to conquer and administer remote African and Asia territories. Similarly, economic and technical superiority allowed the British to intimidate and coerce the Ottoman and Chinese Empires. Although this interpretation has largely been developed within the framework of British history, it has also been used by historians of Africa and Asia to condemn Britain's subjugation of non-Western peoples and cultures.

The problem with focusing the history of imperialism on European motives and causes is that it assigns an unwarranted degree of cultural superiority to Britain. At best, it portrays societies on the imperial periphery as helpless victims in their inability to resist British imperialism; at worst, it suggests that the cause of this weakness was some sort of political or cultural failing. Therefore, the key questions relating to imperial history need to be directed away from questions of European motives and to focus on why imperialism in Africa and Asia was even possible. To be sure, by the end of the nineteenth century, Britain had the industrial and military might to vanquish most non-European foes on the battlefield. Yet the conquest and rule of an unwilling population was prohibitively expensive. With a population of approximately 42 million people at the beginning of the twentieth century, Britain had little chance of holding together an overseas empire of 400 million solely by force of arms. Since Britain lacked the inclination, resources, and manpower to hold its imperial possessions by military force alone, the success of the imperial enterprise depended on its ability to win the cooperation of at least a segment of the subject population.

British imperialists usually secured this cooperation by exploiting social and economic divisions in African and Asian societies. To those groups and individuals willing to participate in the imperial enterprise, British rule and influence offered useful political alliances, new products, access to new markets, employment, Western education, and general social advancement. On the other hand, imperialism usually involved the forceful loss of sovereignty, the destruction or transformation of existing economic systems, institutionalized underdevelopment, and the delegitimization of existing codes of morality and social order. Thus understanding the true causes of British imperialism requires paying close attention to its conflicting impact on subject peoples.

The reinterpretation of imperial history from a world perspective also calls into question conventional assumptions about the global impact of British imperialism. In addition to introducing new political institutions, British rule and informal influence radically restructured African and Asian societies through the introduction of new peoples, technologies, products, languages, and religions. Imperialism also spread plants, animals, and microbes that transformed the ecology and environment of the host colony and often sparked virulent epidemics leading to considerable loss of life. Yet British rule did not wipe the slate clean. Britain's subject populations often retained many of their precolonial institutions and adapted British imperial culture to suit local circumstances.

Furthermore, even though many older histories of metropolitan Britain scarcely mentioned the empire, it is clear that Britain's colonial possessions influenced the development of a new imperial culture by introducing the British public to new languages, products, and values. India was the most influential imperial territory due to its size and vast economic potential, and the cultures and institutions spread around the globe by British imperialism were often more Indian than British. At the very least, this new imperial culture captured the popular imagination of late nineteenth-century Britain and produced new styles of literature, music, art, and decoration. Thus imperialism did not entirely recast African and Asian societies in the British image. Rather, it diffused the peoples and cultures of the empire throughout the world. As we shall see in chapter 5, the imperial century produced a hybrid imperial culture that was largely British in character but not entirely British in style.

2

THE IMPERIAL CENTURY

B ritain's motives in seeking control and influence in non-Western
societies changed considerably during the course of the imperial
century. In the wake of thirty years of warfare that left their continental
rivals in political and economic disarray, the British emerged from the
end of the Napoleonic Wars in 1814 as the world's premier industrial
and commercial power. Although this economic process sent it to the
far corners of the globe in search of markets and raw materials in the
mid-nineteenth century, Britain could rely on free trade and informal
influence to protect its interests because it had the playing field essentially all to itself.

The era of British economic supremacy lasted from the early nineteenth century until the 1870s, when Britain's newly industrialized European rivals turned their attention overseas. Faced with increased (and
largely unexpected) pressure from competition, Britain moved to acquire formal control over regions of the world that it deemed economically or strategically important. British imperialists still preferred the
economy of formal influence to the expense of direct administration. Yet
in cases in which they saw no alternative to formal rule, they suddenly
faced the difficult task of governing millions of non-European subjects
with whom they had little in common. Thus British policy in the imperial century shifted from the older mercantilistic style of imperialism that
survived until the end of the Napoleonic Wars to the era of informal
imperial influence in the mid-nineteenth century, and finally to the
grudging embrace of formal empire in the early 1880s.

SETTLEMENT COLONIES AND THE
TRANSFORMATION OF THE OLD EMPIRE

Britain's first empire consisted largely of holdings in India, South Africa, the West Indies, and North America, which it won during the seventeenth and eighteenth centuries. From an economic standpoint, it was organized along mercantilistic principles, which assumed that colonies existed primarily for the economic benefit of the imperial metropole. Mercantilists measured a nation's wealth by its holdings of gold and silver. They sought to conserve precious metal reserves through regulated trade in which colonies supplied raw materials in return for finished products manufactured in the home country. In the eighteenth century, Britain enforced this closed system through exclusive tariffs and legal preferences like the Navigation Laws, which required important American colonial products (cotton, sugar, tobacco, and indigo) to be exported to British ports on British ships. Most of Britain's overseas commerce was carried out by the British East India Company and other chartered companies, which paid the Crown for an exclusive monopoly on all forms of trade in a given region. These restrictive and unequal systems of exchange engendered considerable hostility among colonists in North America and were a primary cause of the American Revolution.

Growing opposition to mercantilism also mounted in metropolitan Britain at the beginning of the imperial century. The mechanization of textile and hardware production allowed British manufacturers to turn out large quantities of goods much more cheaply than their competitors. Generally speaking, the French, Germans, and Americans did not begin to industrialize until the 1830s and 1840s. Although this head start expanded and enriched the great industrial cities of Manchester, Sheffield, and Birmingham in central and northern Britain, it also made the British economy increasingly dependent on international trade. Since British consumers could not absorb their country's increased industrial output, manufacturers had to look to foreign markets. Furthermore, the British textile industry, which accounted for almost half of Britain's total exports in the 1840s, was almost entirely dependent on imports of raw cotton. Thus Britain's economic health in the early to middle nineteenth century was linked to unfettered international commerce.

Mercantilism's restrictive system of tariffs and monopolies was incompatible with Britain's new emphasis on free markets. Reformers like

Richard Cobden, a radical Member of Parliament, worked to repeal the Corn Laws, which protected privileged agricultural interests by inflating food prices through restrictions on imports of inexpensive foreign grain. Cobden and his supporters allied themselves with industrialists and merchants who were growing equally frustrated with government interference in the free flow of commerce. In 1834 this coalition helped repeal the Navigation Acts and in the 1840s, the Corn Laws. These measures played a role in nearly tripling the volume and value of British trade by 1860. On the other hand, the influx of cheap grain severely damaged the British agricultural sector, and by the late nineteenth century Britain was heavily dependent on imported food.

Thus Britain's security and economic prosperity depended on its ability to balance foreign sales of its manufactured goods with its purchases of food and raw materials. When the volume of Britain's imports surpassed its exports of manufactured goods, the nation relied on service industries to balance its accounts. These "invisible exports" included shipping, insurance, engineering, and international banking. Britain also depended heavily on returns from investments in the developing economies of Europe and North America. Although these factors transformed London into the world's premier center of banking and finance over the course of the imperial century, they reinforced Britain's dependence on the free flow of commerce and capital.

In addition to being committed to free trade, reformers attacked the institution of slavery as an unfree form of labor. In this struggle they were joined by Christian evangelicals, who viewed slavery as immoral, and a faction of British Conservatives who considered it dishonorable. Britain's abolitionist campaign was led by Thomas Fowell Buxton's Society for the Extinction of the Slave Trade and was centered largely in the northern industrial cities, where almost half a million people signed petitions calling for an end to the slave trade. This effort succeeded in banning the transport of slaves on British ships in 1807 and won the total abolition of slavery on British territory in 1833. These changes undermined the profitability of Britain's sugar-producing colonies. British slave owners in the West Indies and on the Indian Ocean island of Mauritius received over £20 million in compensation from the British government for the loss of their human "property" but were faced with the difficult prospect of transforming the former slaves into a sufficiently disciplined paid workforce.

These political and economic changes transformed Britain's first overseas empire. The loss of the thirteen North American colonies demonstrated the political danger of trying to force British settlers to remain within the mercantile system, and the abolition of slavery and the adoption of free trade raised serious questions about the overall value of the remaining colonies. With the exception of India, which still generated considerable revenue from land taxes, the old colonies appeared to cost more than they were worth.

This was particularly true in West Africa, since the robust disease environment in Sierra Leone, the Gambia, Lagos, and the Gold Coast made extensive European settlement a virtual impossibility. Long known as the "white man's grave," the West African coast was home to a host of endemic diseases, including dysentery, typhoid, yellow fever, and malaria. More than three quarters of the British soldiers of the Royal Africa Corps stationed in the Gambia and the Gold Coast between 1819 and 1836 died of disease, and only a handful of the survivors were sufficiently fit for further duty. Most British imperialists therefore avoided extended stays in West Africa until medical advances in the mid-nineteenth century made the region more habitable for Europeans.

As for the remaining colonies in North America and Australia, Britain's growing industrial and commercial supremacy so diminished the threat of foreign competition that British politicians found it easy to shift the burden of local administration to local settler populations. In North America, the British government sought to correct some of the problems that led to the American Revolution by granting limited representative government to its remaining colonies in Upper Canada (Ontario) and Lower Canada (Quebec), New Brunswick, Newfoundland, Nova Scotia, and Prince Edward Island. By rewarding the approximately 40,000 loyalist refugees from the original thirteen colonies with land grants and encouraging increased immigration from Britain, British officials also hoped to assimilate the population of the former French colony of Lower Canada. They also hoped that representative government would give both French and English speakers a greater incentive to remain within the British imperial sphere.

Immigration increased the population of British North America from 250,000 people in 1791 to more than 1.5 million just six decades later. As a result, population pressure in the eastern colonies drove the western settlement of the Northwest Territories, which were the reserve of the Hudson's Bay Company, a chartered company that held a royal monopoly on the region's lucrative fur trade. In the Pacific Northwest, Vancouver Island was the first territory to slip from Company control in the 1840s, and twenty years later survey parties of scientists and geographers deemed the Canadian prairie suitable for settlement and intense cultivation.

In the South Pacific a similar pattern of expansion and settlement took place in Australia at the beginning of the imperial century. The initial colonization of the territories of New South Wales and Tasmania in the late eighteenth century was driven primarily by an effort to empty Britain's crowded jails by deporting criminals overseas. The British government favored transportation (as the practice came to be known) because it offered a "humane" alternative to capital punishment, which was a common penalty for a host of minor crimes in eighteenth-century Britain. It also provided a source of cheap labor for the handful of free settlers who followed the deportees to Australia. On the whole, approximately 160,000 men, women, and children were sent to Australia as convicts by the 1860s.

Although the rate of transportation declined as humanitarians and abolitionists attacked the practice as a form of slavery, the initial wave of forced penal immigration was augmented by almost 100,000 free settlers who took advantage of sponsored colonization programs beginning in the 1830s. They were joined by a following wave of prospectors drawn by the gold rush of 1851. British officials in London had little interest in devoting their limited resources to subsidizing settlers, but individual colonial governments in Australia offered cash bounties to attract a better type of settler. Hoping to create a class of self-reliant yeoman farmers, they offered bounties of as much as £30 to encourage young, respectable married couples to emigrate. On the other end of the spectrum, imperial propagandist Edward Gibbon Wakefield sought to re-create the rural British gentry in the colonies by raising land prices to create a class of wealthy landholders and a subordinate class of tenants. Neither plan came to full fruition, but together they accelerated the rate of free settlement substantially by diminishing Australia's reputation as a land of convicts.

Finally, New Zealand was the only significant new settlement colony that Britain acquired over the course of the imperial century. British explorers, whalers, and merchants had regular contacts with New

Zealand dating back to the mid-eighteenth century, but the presence of the Maori, a numerous, well-organized, and militaristic people, made the islands an unsuitable site for a British penal colony. The few British traders and missionaries who settled in New Zealand before the imperial century did so under the protection of local Maori chiefs rather than the Crown.

The British government did very little to directly encourage the formal settlement and colonization of New Zealand. It willingly stood by while the initial efforts of private companies to settle the territory failed as a result of Maori hostility and opposition from the humanitarian lobby in Britain, and it was not until 1839 that Edward Gibbon Wakefield's New Zealand Colonization Company finally established a permanent settlement on the North Island. The rate of immigration increased dramatically once this foothold was firmly established, and by 1850 the British population of New Zealand numbered approximately 25,000 people.

Yet the mere presence of large numbers of British settlers was not enough to force the British government to overcome its unwillingness to incur the cost of adding territory to its formal empire. Interestingly enough, New Zealand became a British protectorate because British missionaries and the local British Resident (who had no official authority) succeeded in convincing the Colonial Office that the growing community of merchants, whalers, seal hunters, military deserters, and land speculators threatened to plunge the islands into anarchy. In 1840, local officials persuaded Maori leaders to become British subjects in return for vague guarantees that they would retain title to their land. In practice, the Treaty of Waitangi, as the agreement came to be known, allowed British land speculators to exploit Maori institutions of communal land tenure by buying or seizing large sections of the North Island. The Maori clashed with the British army in the 1860s in an attempt to stem the rising tide of settlers, but their inevitable defeat gave the settler leaders an excuse to seize an additional 3 million acres of land from the "treasonous" rebels.

It should be kept in mind, however, that colonial officials in London had no direct interest in dispossessing the Maori. The settlers and land speculators succeeded in transforming New Zealand into a crown colony by compelling the British government to protect the lives and property of British citizens. In doing so, they maneuvered Britain into acquiring a new settlement colony at a time when most British imperialists had little desire to add remote overseas regions to their formal empire.

Faced with the expense of administering and defending its growing settlement colonies in North America, Australia, and New Zealand, the British government began to explore ways to allow the settlers to take more responsibility for managing their local affairs. Under what became known as "responsible government" it made the royal governors and ministers of those colonies with sufficient economical maturity and financial stability responsible to a locally elected assembly. In granting responsible government to the North American colonies beginning in the 1840s, British officials were partially motivated by fears that the slow pace of political progress might inspire them to seek annexation by the United States. With a precedent firmly established, they extended the same privilege to New Zealand and Australian colonies a decade later (although the governor of New Zealand retained responsibility for dealing with the Maori).

With responsible government firmly established, the British government also encouraged the various colonies in North America and Australia to join together in larger political units to foster even greater self-sufficiency in economic development and defense. In 1867, the colonies of Upper and Lower Canada, Nova Scotia, and New Brunswick combined to form the nucleus of modern Canada. The new confederation facilitated westward expansion and reduced the chance that Britain might have to protect its North American colonies from a hostile United States angered by British support for the South during the U.S. Civil War. The Australian territories did not join together until 1901, when the threat of German and French expansion in the South Pacific convinced the individual colonies to surrender their autonomy to a larger federation. The British government retained control of both Australian and Canadian international relations and had the prerogative of vetoing discriminatory tariffs on British imports.

Britain was less willing to grant responsible government to its African territories and the West Indian sugar colonies. Concerned about the southern African Cape Colony's treatment of its non-European population, British officials granted the territory "representative" rather than "responsible" government in 1853. Under this system, the British governor retained a greater degree of authority over a locally elected assembly. Conversely, the Caribbean planters voluntarily surrendered their right to responsible government to the Colonial Office in the 1860s because they were afraid of being swamped by a non-European electorate composed largely of freed slaves.

THE ERA OF INFORMAL EMPIRE

Britain's imperial policy in the mid-nineteenth century was shaped largely by confidence in its industrial and commercial might. Free trade advocates assumed that the mutual benefits of unfettered commerce would usher in an era of world peace. Britain avoided the wave of revolutions that swept across Europe in the 1830s and 1840s, and the final defeat of Napoleon virtually eliminated the French naval threat to Britain's overseas trade. In fact, Britain's ability to embrace a policy of free trade and informal imperialism was almost entirely due to the lack of serious foreign rivals. British governments could make up for the budget deficits that resulted from the end of protectionist legislation and high tariffs only by cutting defense costs. Thus, even though Britain was the world's only global military power during the imperial century, its prosperity was largely dependent on world peace.

British politicians were continually forced to weigh the use of military action against the forced economy brought on by their commitment to low tariffs and free trade. These stringent economic realities sparked an intense debate in British imperial and political circles over the worth of formal empire. Although few questioned the value of British India, Richard Cobden, John Bright, and other free trade enthusiasts of what became known as the Manchester School argued that Britain's remaining dependent colonies were an unnecessary expense. They were willing to sanction the use of force only to compel non-European states and societies to open their markets to British trade.

A few of the most extreme opponents of formal empire argued that Britain should actually abandon its most expensive overseas holdings. In 1865, Sir Charles Adderley stood in Parliament to attack Britain's small West African colonies for their inability to contribute to the cost of imperial defense. He charged that the value of British trade in these territories did not offset the cost of their administration and complained that tensions with local African rulers drew Britain into unnecessary and ex-

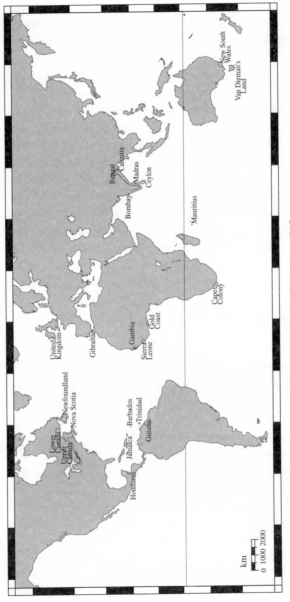

Map 2.1 The British Empire, c. 1815

pensive conflicts. In response to Adderley's criticisms, Parliament convened a special committee, which recommended withdrawal from all West African territories except the colony of liberated slaves in Sierra Leone.

Although the committee's proposals never came to pass, they illustrated the widespread indifference (if not outright hostility) of many influential British politicians toward formal empire. In spite of this official resistance to acquiring new dependencies, the British Empire grew at a rate of nearly 100,000 square miles per year during the mid-nineteenth century. With the exception of the relatively insignificant Greek Ionian Islands, Britain did not surrender a single acre of overseas territory during this period. Although most British imperialists may have resisted taking on the financial burden of governing new colonies, they were not opposed to acquiring small strategically or economically important islands and bases like the Falklands off the coast of Argentina, Aden on the tip of Arabia, and the port of Hong Kong in coastal China. Britain also expanded and consolidated its hold over India during the era of informal empire.

Furthermore, British commercial and political leaders were usually willing to use military force to expand their informal economic and social influence overseas. Britain's Opium Wars with China in 1839 and 1856 were intended primarily to force the Chinese to end their restrictions on British trade. Lord Palmerston, the British prime minister, justified these wars as the defense of free trade and downplayed the fact that the most lucrative British export to China was Indian opium. In 1845, Britain defeated Argentinean attempts to monopolize trade on the River Plate by blockading the river with Royal Navy gunboats.

British imperialists were also willing to use force simply to demonstrate that there were serious repercussions to wounding Britain's pride. In 1867, the British government sent an expedition of over 13,000 British and Indian soldiers into Ethiopia to punish King Theodorus for taking two minor British diplomats hostage. Costing over £8 million, the operation accomplished very little because British forces simply withdrew from the country after inflicting a decisive defeat upon the Ethiopians.

For the most part, however, British imperialists preferred to reap the benefits of informal influence rather than resort to expensive military operations to convince non-Western nations to surrender key aspects of their sovereignty. Wherever possible, they preferred to work through existing political institutions. In South America, Britain abandoned plans to annex the estuary of the River Plate as unrealistically expensive and concentrated instead on using its influence to induce the Latin Americans to restructure their economies to favor British interests. British commercial concerns dominated South American markets, and British investors were the main creditors of the debt-ridden Argentine and Brazilian governments. In the latter half of the imperial century, they owned almost 50 percent of Argentina's fixed capital assets. These factors gave Britain such a considerable degree of influence in Latin America that formal imperial control was unnecessary.

Similarly, Britain's goal in its relations with the Ottoman and Chinese Empires was to achieve a maximum degree of influence without having to incur the cost and responsibility of direct administration. The Ottoman Empire was an important buffer state that prevented Russia, Britain's main central Asian rival, from threatening the routes to India. China, on the other hand, had little strategic value, but influential British industrialists and traders fantasized about the millions of potential customers waiting to buy British products if only the Chinese government could be persuaded to open its markets.

Therefore British imperialists sought to erode the sovereignty of these great non-European empires just enough to make their political and economic institutions more open. On the other hand, too much interference threatened to produce political disintegration, economic instability, and a potentially dangerous power vacuum that would force Britain to resort to formal annexation. British imperialists therefore hoped to strengthen these "rotten empires" by convincing them to adopt constitutions, free trade, industrial technology, and Western-style education. Few realized that in many ways their cure was worse than the disease. The loss of sovereignty inherent in informal influence, plus the imposition of Western culture and institutions, invariably exacerbated simmering social and political tensions in many non-Western societies.

Throughout the imperial century, the increasingly influential British evangelical movement disseminated Christianity and Western values, which also expanded Britain's informal influence. Many of Britain's Protestant denominations underwent a popular religious revival in the late eighteenth century. Believing that industrial and political change had produced a moral crisis in the country, they worked to transform Britain into a sufficiently Christian nation. Their highest priority was universal spiritual salvation, which in practical terms meant spreading the knowledge of God and saving the emerging British working class from the evils of drink and sexual license. As has already been noted, they also joined with free trade reformers to condemn the evils of slavery.

Most Evangelicals were not opposed to imperialism and attributed Britain's power and influence overseas to the success of its divine mission. They felt a profound sense of obligation to share Christianity and British civilization with the "less fortunate" non-European peoples of the world. To a large degree, they equated difference with backwardness and considered cultures different from their own as representing an earlier, almost childlike stage of development. Although these views now seem unacceptably biased and judgmental, most Evangelicals believed they had a moral duty to protect and nurture "backward" societies. Many sought to prove that their African and Asian disciples were capable of civilization and founded schools and hospitals to share the benefits of European culture.

Evangelicals supported the efforts of Thomas Buxton, who emphasized the humane development of Africa as part of his campaign to abolish slavery. In the 1830s, Buxton was active in the Aborigines Protection Society and chaired a parliamentary committee which concluded that free labor brought the same benefits as free trade. Buxton placed most of the blame for slavery on African society and argued that the emancipation of slaves in British territories had to be accompanied by the total elimination of the institution of slavery in Africa. This goal could be accomplished only by providing Africans with a sufficiently lucrative alternative to trafficking in slaves. Buxton and his allies therefore popularized the concept of "legitimate commerce," whereby Africans would turn their energies to the production of the tropical commodities required by industrial Britain. Hence formal British rule would not be needed to coerce Africans into taking part in this enterprise because both sides would reap the mutual benefits of increased trade.

Most British evangelicals concurred with these sentiments, believing that commerce carried the message of salvation. They founded the London Missionary Society, the Church Missionary Society, the British Bible Society, the Church of Scotland Mission, and other missionary organizations to spread their message of Christianity, industry, and commerce overseas. Although these missions were geared primarily to producing Christian converts, they also spread British values and culture through the media of Western education and medical care. Missionaries often differed with the proponents of informal influence and free trade when they encountered cultural practices or political institutions that they deemed barbarous or uncivilized. In these cases they were quite willing to argue for British intervention and even formal annexation on humanitarian grounds. Some historians have accused the missionary societies of painting an overly lurid picture of non-Western "barbarism" to raise funds and attract followers in Britain. Their ability to mobilize widespread support among the newly literate British middle classes for overseas humanitarian causes certainly helped defeat Adderley's calls for withdrawal from West Africa and provided a cover of legitimacy for future British territorial annexations in Africa and Asia.

BRITAIN AND THE "NEW" IMPERIALISM

Although Britain's rapid acquisition of extensive territories in Africa and Asia in the late nineteenth century appeared to be a sudden and radical departure from its preference for informal influence, many historians have argued that the shift to formal imperial control was primarily Britain's response to increased economic and political competition from its European rivals. Its prosperity and economic strength was built on its industrial head start and isolation from the turbulent affairs of the continent. Yet these advantages came at a price. Without serious competition, the British had little incentive to modernize their industrial base and remained heavily dependent on simple manufactures, including textiles, iron, and hardware goods. British industry also did not take advantage of innovations in production. Britain's profitable exports of technology and capital helped its German and American rivals take the lead in the manufacture of chemicals, electrical goods, and steel. In 1870 Britain accounted for roughly one-third of the world's industrial output, but by 1914 this figure had fallen to only one-seventh.

Furthermore, as was the case with most industrial powers, the British economy's reliance on manufacturing made it vulnerable to cycles of high economic prosperity and depression. Generally speaking, Britain experienced an economic downturn every seven to ten years. Although most of these crises were followed by periods of profitable recovery, the

Great Depression of 1873 was so severe that many feared it would never end. The factors that produced the depression were complex, but its primary cause was the increased industrial capacity of Britain's American and European rivals. In other words, there simply were not enough consumers to purchase their manufactures. This surplus production drove down prices, diminished opportunities for profitable investment, and created widespread unemployment.

Many in Britain blamed the depression on the high protective tariffs that rival powers used to defend their developing industrial bases from British competition. In 1885 the Royal Commission on the Depression of Trade Industry concluded that foreigners had abused the principles of open commerce by using state support to secure an unfair advantage over British manufacturers and traders, who were still playing by the rules. Although the British economy had largely recovered by the beginning of the twentieth century, the depression of 1873 led some British imperialists to question the value of informal empire.

Britain's economic anxieties were compounded by its growing sense of military insecurity. After the Crimean War of 1855–1856, Russia's army of over half a million men appeared to threaten British India at a time when the Indian Mutiny of 1857 raised serious doubts about the reliability of the Indian army. In 1906 the commander in chief of British forces in India estimated that he would need 160,000 British troops to counter a Russian invasion, with an additional 300,000 to 400,000 reinforcements in the following year. Thus when France and Germany reemerged as major continental powers in the 1870s, British generals began to fear that they were stretched too thinly around the globe. To further complicate matters, Britain was already devoting over a third of its budget to the military and had the highest defense spending per capita of any European nation in the late nineteenth century.

Therefore Britain reorganized its armed forces in an effort to simultaneously reduce defense spending and counter its new imperial rivals. In 1870, Edward T. Cardwell, secretary of state for war, concentrated the regular British army in India and Britain by withdrawing troops from the colonies. Cardwell also ordered an overall force reduction of 25,000 men, so that in 1881 the British army numbered only 70,000 regular soldiers. By necessity, Britain relied on the Royal Navy and locally recruited colonial forces (most of whom were non-European) to defend its overseas empire.

These mounting economic and military concerns produced a profound crisis of confidence in British economic and political circles. Britain's imperialists understood that their empire depended on world peace and the unrestricted flow of commerce and investment. As tensions with their continental rivals mounted, they began to fear that they were entering into an era of imperial decline. Faced with the prospect of suffering the same fate as the Romans, British imperialists adopted a siege mentality focused on defending their global interests.

This change of thinking was particularly apparent in British politics. Apart from a commitment to protecting global free trade, British Liberals and Conservatives were largely unconcerned with imperial issues before the Great Depression of the 1870s. Both parties lamented the unfortunate circumstances that compelled Britain to annex new overseas territories and disagreed only over the timing and methods of these acquisitions. The Reform Bills of 1867 and 1884 broadened the British electorate and tempted politicians to use the empire to shape public opinion and win votes. Liberal prime minister William Gladstone framed imperial issues in high moral terms while Benjamin Disraeli, the leader of the Conservatives, used the empire to attract working-class voters by promoting national pride. His successor, the earl of Salisbury, was a strong advocate of defensive imperialism who worked actively to expand the empire. Joseph Chamberlain, Salisbury's colonial secretary from 1895 to 1902, believed that popular imperialism was the best cure for Britain's growing social and class tensions. In a sharp break with the official commitment to free trade, he argued for an imperial customs union that would use tariffs and preferences to deny Britain's rivals access to its colonial markets.

Although Chamberlain's proposal never came to pass, the Great Depression transformed many of Britain's manufacturing and commercial leaders into unabashed protectionists who hoped to solve the problem of overproduction by expanding their markets. Angered that their competitors had flaunted the "natural" laws of free trade, they pressed their leaders to intervene forcefully to protect existing markets and open new ones. These industrialists naturally focused on Britain's captive economy in India but also called for the acquisition of the hinterlands of Africa to fend off potential rivals. Some historians have argued that British manufacturers were too provincial to have much political influence in the gentlemanly circles of power in London, but their calls for the defensive annexation of potentially valuable overseas territories struck a popular chord.

Over the course of the nineteenth century Britain's governing class of landed elites became increasingly allied with London financiers and investors. As the decline of British agriculture forced many aristocrats to seek new sources of wealth, London's financiers and merchant bankers became the logical partners for the gentry because they were products of the public school system and had sufficient leisure and wealth to support an aristocratic lifestyle. These gentlemanly capitalists directed a London-based international trading and financial system. They raised profitable loans for foreign governments, invested heavily in the infrastructure of developing economies, and provided credit to British merchants. Although returns on these foreign investments were not much higher than domestic levels, Britain's internal economy in the late nineteenth century simply could not provide enough profitable outlets for its excess capital. As a result, from 1865 to 1914, Britain's foreign investment amounted to about two-thirds of its approximately £5 billion in total savings.

Therefore British gentlemanly capitalists depended on an integrated global economy that allowed for the free flow of international commerce and investment. Unlike British industrialists, they did not see the need to extend Britain's formal empire to protect its markets. Territorial control was usually unimportant as long as their investments were safe. Nevertheless, they did not oppose the growth of the British Empire in the late nineteenth century. British investors profited from expansion, and even though less than 10 percent of Britain's total savings went to its non-self-governing colonies, the acquisition of new territory in Africa and Asia broadened the scope of the global British economic system.

The main difference between this "new" imperialism of formal empire and the midcentury empire of informal influence was that it took force to adapt African and Asian economies to the requirements of British commerce and investment. Although there were few opportunities for profitable investment in these underdeveloped economies, substantial profits could be made from the guaranteed loans and subsidies that the British government used to convince well-connected investors to risk their money in the new, less lucrative corners of the empire.

In addition to these economic factors, Britain's shift to formal empire in the late nineteenth century was abetted by shifting social attitudes

that made it easier to conquer and administer non-European populations. In imperial circles, the evangelical zeal of the missionary movement was drowned out by Social Darwinism and pseudoscientific racism. Although Charles Darwin did not apply his theory of natural
selection and evolution to human societies, the publication of *The Origin
of Species* in 1859 had a profound influence on imperialist thought. British Social Darwinists concluded that "less fit" non-European peoples
were incapable of coping with modernity and were unable to recognize
the merits of Britain's superior culture because they were at a lower stage
of evolutionary development. By this line of reasoning, "blackness" was
equated with backwardness. The Social Darwinists developed new aca-
demic disciplines that used the pseudoscientific study of craniology and
comparative anatomy to "prove" the inferiority of Africans and Asians.

On the basis of these specious arguments, British imperialists decided they had a paternalistic duty to rule non-European peoples because
they were incapable of governing themselves. Although some missionaries remained committed to culturally transforming Africa and Asia along
European lines, the public mood in Britain shifted after the 1857 Indian
Mutiny. The 1865 revolt of ex-slaves in Jamaica confirmed the assumption that non-Europeans were incapable of civilization.

British imperialists were confident in their cultural superiority because the technical advances of the late-nineteenth-century industrial
revolution had made it relatively easy for them to extend their influence
to the tropical regions of the world. The discovery that microbes caused
disease and that quinine, which was extracted from the bark of the South
American cinchona tree, offered some protection from malaria and made
tropical Africa far less threatening (and deadly) to Westerners. Whereas
death rates among Europeans in their first year of residency in West Africa were 250 to 750 per thousand before 1840, by the end of the century, they had dropped to just fifty to one hundred per thousand. The
steamship and the railway opened African and Asian hinterlands to conquest and commerce, and a new global network of undersea telegraph
cables allowed London to exercise greater administrative control over
the far corners of the empire. Before 1850, officials in India needed two
to three months to send and receive messages via ship and train from
Britain; by the 1870s it took only a day to exchange telegrams on the
submarine cable system.

As impressive as these advances in medicine and communication

were, no innovation did more to shift the balance of power between Europe and the non-Western world than development of modern military technology. Armored British gunboats blockaded Chinese ports during the Opium Wars, forcing African merchants and rulers to tolerate open British trade on the Niger River. The repeating rifle, the rapid-fire maxim gun, and the explosive field artillery shell all made it relatively inexpensive for a handful of British soldiers to defeat a non-European enemy that greatly outnumbered them. Although this arms gap was less pronounced in Asia, it was devastating in Africa. In 1898, British forces at the Battle of Omdurman killed approximately 11,000 Sudanese in five hours at a cost of only twenty British and Egyptian soldiers.

The ease with which Britain won these appallingly lopsided battles seemed to vindicate the Social Darwinists. Yet it was all too easy to mistake military dominance for cultural superiority. British imperial enthusiasts failed to realize that although it may have been easy to defeat a poorly equipped non-European foe, it was quite another thing to rule them without resorting to a protracted and expensive period of military occupation.

If British imperialists were blind to this fact, it was because they acquired enormous tracts of territory in Africa and Asia with very little effort in the late nineteenth century. Britain was an active participant in the European partition of Africa in the 1880s. In addition to expanded coastal holdings in West Africa, Britain's share of the spoils included Egypt, the Sudan, and British Somaliland in Northeast Africa; Zanzibar, Uganda, and what came to be known as Kenya in East Africa; Nyasaland (Malawi), Northern Rhodesia (Zambia), and Southern Rhodesia (Zimbabwe) in central Africa; and Swaziland, Basutoland (Lesotho), and Bechuanaland (Botswana) in southern Africa. It took a protracted war with the Afrikaners (1899–1902) to consolidate British rule over South Africa. In Asia, Britain strengthened the frontiers of India by occupying Burma and what is now Pakistan. It acquired sovereignty over most of the states in the Malay Peninsula by 1896 and occupied numerous islands in the South Pacific between 1874 and the end of the nineteenth century.

Although Britain did not acquire extensive Ottoman and Chinese territory during this period, its relations with these non-European empires changed dramatically under the "new" imperialism. Its occupation of Egypt in 1882 and incorporation of the Persian Gulf states into the British sphere of influence diminished the strategic importance of the Ottoman Empire as a buffer state again Russian expansionism. British financiers came to consider the Ottomans a bad risk, and politicians like Prime Minister Lord Salisbury began to openly discuss the need to abandon the older "dying nations."

China, on the other hand, was still attractive to British merchants and investors at the end of the nineteenth century. Yet the potential dismemberment of the Chinese Empire by its European rivals forced Britain to abandon its earlier reliance on informal influence to protect its economic interests. The British government therefore took part in the European "scramble for concessions" in China in 1897 and pegged out the Yangtze River valley as a specifically British sphere of influence. In addition, it leased the port of Weihaiwei for twenty-five years and added the Kowloon New Territories to Hong Kong under a ninety-nine-year lease.

CONSOLIDATION OF EMPIRE

By the beginning of the twentieth century, the British Empire had essentially reached its full territorial extent. Although British imperialists often compared themselves to their Roman predecessors, the former organized their empire along substantially different lines. The British Empire was never a single administrative entity, and it lacked a uniform language, religion, and code of laws. The currency of both metropolitan Britain and the Australasian settlement colonies was gold-based sterling. India and British East Africa used silver rupees, whereas Malaya had silver dollars. Britain's colonies did not adopt a uniform sterling exchange standard until the eve of the First World War. In reality, the British Empire was a decentralized conglomeration of diverse territories and cultures whose only common point of reference was interaction with British imperial authority.

The effective administration of such a heterogeneous mix of peoples was no easy matter. There was never an "Imperial Department" of the British government; the Foreign Office, India Office, War Office, Colonial Office, Admiralty, and Board of Trade shared responsibility for running the empire. Nevertheless, most of the territories acquired under the

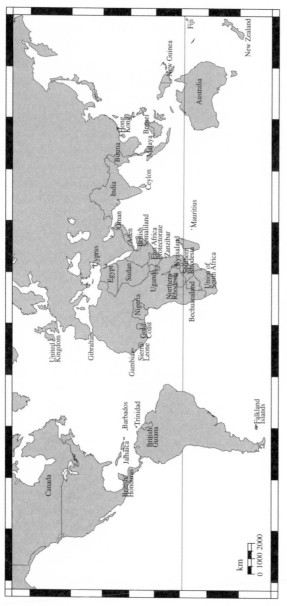

Map 2.2   The British Empire, c. 1914

"new" imperialism were administered by either the Foreign Office or the Colonial Office. Colonial matters were largely an afterthought to the Foreign Office, and the Colonial Office was surprisingly weak and understaffed during the imperial century. In 1907, its London office employed slightly more than one hundred people.

The colonies themselves were governed through a bewildering array of administrative systems, which were due more to local improvisation than any coherent philosophy of imperial rule. As has already been noted, the older settlement colonies enjoyed responsible or representative government. The British East India Company did not give way to an Indian council presided over by a member of the British cabinet until 1858. The other territories that had non-European majorities were usually designated as crown colonies under the autocratic authority of a royal governor who was the personal representative of the British monarch. Most of the colonies acquired during the partition of Africa became protectorates under the initial authority of the Foreign Office. Under this system, local rulers technically retained their sovereignty under the "protection" of the Crown, but most eventually saw their territories transformed into crown colonies when transferred to Colonial Office control.

In practice, many British possessions fell outside these relatively straightforward administrative categories. Egypt was run by a British consul general, who was theoretically an adviser to the Egyptian cabinet. The Sarawak protectorate in northern Borneo was ruled by a hereditary British raja, British Somaliland had a commissioner responsible to the Indian government, and Ascension Island was run by a captain in the Royal Navy. In terms of British administrative personnel, the Colonial Office's entire field staff was slightly less than 6,000 strong, and all of India was governed by the civil service, which numbered just 3,000 men (including a handful of Indians) at the turn of the twentieth century.

Although Britain had its own strong domestic tradition of decentralized rule, its diverse imperial administrative policies were inspired largely by pragmatic adaptations to the strict financial limitations that its Treasury Department placed on imperial spending. Britain's commitment to free trade precluded revenue-generating tariffs and shifted the financial burden of government to the British taxpayer. The cost of protecting a global empire forced Britain to spend more per capita on defense than any other European power. Thus the Treasury was absolutely adamant that the colonies assume the cost of their own administration. It had absolute authority over foreign and domestic spending, and any colonial government needing financial assistance from the British government had to submit to the Treasury's ruthless insistence on economy and financial restraint.

These fiscal limitations had a profound influence on the character and scope of British colonial administration. Although Britain could, if it chose, defeat virtually any non-European foe on the battlefield, it could not afford the high cost of prolonged wars of attrition or widespread civil insurrection. For example, the colonial government of Sierra Leone had to spend £45,000 to suppress the Hut Tax Rebellion of 1898. On a larger scale, punitive operations in the East Africa Protectorate (Kenya) between 1895 and 1905 cost roughly one-third of the protectorate's total public spending for that period. Furthermore, the 70,000-man regular British army was not large enough to provide occupation forces for every territory in the empire with a non-European majority. Therefore even though Britain had a tremendous amount of coercive force at its disposal, it could not afford to provoke widespread discontent and unrest among its colonial subjects.

The image of the omnipotent colonial state with the power to arbitrarily reorder indigenous economic and social institutions is a myth. British imperialists could govern their non-European colonies only with the tacit assent of at least a small segment of the subject population. Britain lacked the resources and personnel to govern its global empire exclusively with European officials, and it recruited Africans and Asians as lower-level clerks, translators, artisans, police officers, and soldiers to help run the colonies.

British imperialists also endeavored to co-opt indigenous elites into the lower levels of the colonial bureaucracy. This system, known as indirect rule, was originally developed in India, as Britain governed much of the subcontinent through Indian princes and rajas. When colonial officials exported indirect rule to Africa, they sought to apply it to African kings and chiefs. Indirect rule lowered the cost of colonial administration by shrinking the British administrative staff and reducing the possibility that foreign rule might provoke unrest. As Nigerian governor Frederick Lugard put it, "It is one thing to excite an ignorant peasantry against an alien usurper, but quite another thing to challenge a native ruler."

Theoretically , these "native rulers" derived their legitimacy from their "traditional" status in precolonial society; in reality British officials often promoted them to positions of authority based on their willingness to participate in the colonial system. Although these British clients often incurred the animosity of their fellow subjects, cooperation had its rewards. Colonial officials relied on these elites to interpret African and Asian society, and thus they had a substantial amount of influence in defining the customs and traditions that became the basis of colonial law. Therefore, subordinate indirect rulers in the British Empire enjoyed a measure of political power, economic security, and social status.

Similarly, in the Ottoman and Chinese Empires Britain relied on a class of translators, managers, commercial agents, and, in some cases, Christian converts to exert its informal influence. These intermediaries often grew wealthy through their partnership with British imperialists. In the eighteenth century, the British East India Company's Indian agents helped dismantle the Mughal Empire. In the nineteenth century, Britain did not have the same designs on the Chinese and Ottoman Empires, but in both cases local allies helped penetrate closed domestic markets by weakening the social consensus that had previously excluded foreigners. Although these activities made both empires dangerously unstable, the Chinese and the Ottomans escaped the fate of the Mughals. The westernized Chinese and Ottoman intermediary classes, wealthy as they were, were not powerful enough to sufficiently undermine the religious and cultural bonds that held their empires together.

These cases demonstrate clearly that the expansion of Britain's formal empire and informal influence into the tropical regions of Africa and Asia was determined by its ability to find partners among the local population. The remaining chapters of this book show that, for the most part, the loss of sovereignty inherent in British imperialism restructured indigenous political, economic, and social institutions in a manner that created considerable hardship for most of Britain's non-European subjects. Yet British imperialism also offered opportunity to at least a small segment of the colonial populace. Chinese commercial agents, Ottoman translators, Indian princes, or African clerks were certainly neither loyal British subjects nor calculating, self-interested traitors. Their participation in the imperial system was based on a rational response to the new realities of direct British rule or, in the case of the Ottoman and Chinese Empires, indirect British influence. Furthermore, the economic austerity of imperialism, which led Britain to seek allies among its African and

Asian subjects, tempered some of the worst abuses of the imperial system and created a medium for the diffusion of ideas between metropolitan Britain and its African and Asian periphery.

SUGGESTIONS FOR FURTHER READING

Cain, P. J., and A. G. Hopkins. *British Imperialism: Innovation and Expansion, 1688–1914.* London: Longmans, 1993.

Davis, Lance, and Robert Huttenback. *Mammon and the Pursuit of Empire: The Political Economy of British Imperialism, 1860–1912.* Cambridge: Cambridge University Press, 1986.

Eldridge, C. C., ed. *British Imperialism in the Nineteenth Century.* New York: St Martin's, 1984.

Fagan, Brian. *Clash of Cultures.* 2d ed. Walnut Creek, Calif.: Alta Mira, 1998.

Hyam, Ronald. *Britain's Imperial Century, 1815–1914: A Study of Empire and Expansion.* New York: Barnes and Noble, 1976.

Hynes, W. G. *The Economics of Empire: Britain, Africa, and the New Imperialism, 1870–1895.* London: Longmans, 1979.

Spiers, Edward. *The Late Victorian Army, 1868–1902.* Manchester: Manchester University Press, 1992.

3

INDIA

India was, without question, the most important and influential of Britain's imperial possessions. As such, it does not fall neatly into the categories of the "old" or "new" imperialism. The British East India Company gained control of India during the eighteenth century, but the territory was so valuable that not even the harshest critic of empire ever suggested abandoning it during the mid-nineteenth century enthusiasm for informal imperialism. Indians paid high taxes, were captive consumers of British products, and served in Britain's colonial army. Although India was subjected to most of the same forces that transformed the British Empire in late nineteenth century, debates over the cause and effect of the "new" imperialism on India have little meaning. Therefore, this chapter examines how Indians reacted to the changing dynamics of empire that transformed British rule in India over the course of the imperial century.

As Britain's first major imperial possession to have a non-European majority, India became the administrative model for British holdings in Africa and other parts of Asia. It would have been impossible to conquer and administer millions of people living in such a vast expanse of territory without the tacit assistance of at least a small segment of the Indian population. Moreover, Britain spread India's peoples, products, and cultures around the globe, and in many ways the resulting overseas empire was almost as Indian as it was British. British rule was a particularly potent force in India because it lasted for nearly two hundred years. Thus India serves as an excellent model of the impact of imperialism on both non-European peoples and the British themselves.

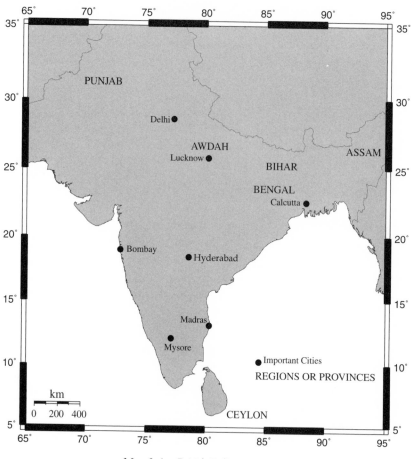

Map 3.1   British India, c. 1914

THE ORIGINS OF BRITISH INDIA

Britain was able to acquire sovereignty over the Indian subcontinent in the eighteenth century because much of it was already ruled by
foreigners. The British supplanted the Mughal Empire, which had subjugated northern India in the sixteenth century. The Mughals were Is-
lamicized Mongols who, like their British successors, governed India by
right of conquest. They ruled the non-Muslim majority by giving Hindu
elites important positions in their army and administration, as well as co-

opting princes, rajas, and village notables at the local level. As one of the world's great imperial powers in the seventeenth century, Mughal India used its wealth and administrative genius to produce impressive achievements in science, art, architecture, and literature. By the eighteenth century, however, the peripheral regions of the empire had begun to break away. Mughal governors and viceroys used their growing autonomy to become feudal rulers in their own right. Most, however, acknowledged the emperor's formal authority and continued to pay him a share of their territories' annual revenues to maintain their legitimacy. Yet as their governors became autonomous rulers, however, the Mughals lost control of some of their most lucrative holdings in Bengal, Awadh, and the Deccan Plateau.

Many historians have attributed the conquest of India to Britain's need to impose order on the decaying Mughal Empire, but it was actually economic opportunity created by the commercialization of the Indian economy that drew Britain into the hinterlands of the subcontinent. One of the great ironies of Indian history is that India was not subjugated by the British government but by a privately held chartered company that paid the Crown for the exclusive right to monopolize British trade with the subcontinent. Although the British East India Company (BEIC) competed with other French and Dutch chartered companies for control of the most lucrative Asian markets, it had no British rivals. The Company, as the BEIC was commonly known, was chartered in 1600 and within a century had leased over twenty trading posts near Madras and Bombay from the Mughal emperor. At first its interests were primarily commercial, but it did not realize substantial profits because it was forced to import silver to pay for indigo, saltpeter, cotton cloth, silk, and spices. Company officials therefore used their private army to sell military protection and collect tribute in the semi-independent Indian territories.

The eastern province of Bengal proved to be the Company's most lucrative field of operations. Although technically under the suzerainty of the emperor, Bengal was governed as a substantially autonomous fiefdom by a Mughal vassal known as a nawab. Bengali merchants grew wealthy by supplying commodities to the Company's main trading settlement at Calcutta, which enhanced the BEIC's influence and alarmed Nawab Siraj-ud Daula. When the Company violated the terms of its lease by fortifying Calcutta against the French, he tried to drive them out by force of arms. Many Calcutta merchants sided with the British in the ensuing conflict, and Company forces under the command of Robert Clive, formerly a clerk, won a major victory over the nawab at the Battle of Plassey in 1757.

As a result, the emperor granted the Company the right to manage the finances and taxes of Bengal, which made the British East India Company his nominal vassals. Bengal was a rich agricultural region, and company officials found that their commission on the annual land tax was much more profitable than trading. Many representatives of the Company amassed great personal fortunes by taking advantage of the monopolies and subsidies that were the perquisites of all Indian rulers in the eighteenth century. As they became more deeply enmeshed in Indian commerce, the Company's influence spread into the interior of the subcontinent.

Therefore the BEIC had a vested interest in maintaining Indian political stability to ensure the free flow of commerce and efficient tax collection. The Company sent military garrisons and special ambassadors, known as residents, to the courts of their most important Indian allies. These rulers were obligated to pay for protection, and the high cost of these garrisons often drove them into bankruptcy. In these cases, company officials subsequently assumed control of their taxes and finances to ensure continued stability. Although these indebted Indian rulers retained a degree of formal autonomy, they became de facto vassals of the Company.

These expansionist policies were largely inspired by the BEIC's economic interests, but the Company also sought to ensure that important Indian rulers did not fall under the sway of their French rivals. Once it finally drove the French out of India (during the Seven Years War in the 1760s) and defeated the powerful Indian states of Mysore and Hyderabad later in the century, the Company emerged as the dominant political and economic power in India. Although the Sikhs and Marathas in central and northwestern India were still independent, there were no serious rivals to challenge BEIC control of the subcontinent.

For the purposes of administration, the Company divided India into the Bengal, Madras, and Bombay presidencies. Although each had its own separate civil service and army, the governor-general of Bengal coordinated Company policy in the subcontinent as the senior British official in India. The BEIC based its legitimacy on its status as a symbolic

Mughal vassal and continued to pay the emperor a nominal sum as symbolic tribute until 1843. In actual fact, however, the Company was directly responsible to the British government in London. As BEIC holdings in India grew more extensive and profitable, Parliament passed the Regulating Act of 1778, the Indian Act of 1784, and the Charter Act of 1793 to assert more formal metropolitan control over company affairs. These acts made the Company responsible to a board of control composed of six unpaid councilors, with the board's president serving in the British cabinet. The new rules also established a professional Indian civil service, staffed by British revenue collectors and district magistrates.

As has already been noted, the Company's primary interest in India shifted from commerce to tax collection over the course of the eighteenth century. Before the arrival of the British, Mughal officials in the province of Bengal extracted one-third of its gross annual produce in land taxes and tribute. After Plassey, these land revenues freed the British East India Company from having to import silver to purchase Indian products and subsidized dividend payments to its stockholders in Britain. Company officials therefore worked to make Indian agriculture more productive and tax collection more efficient.

Under the Mughals, a class of hereditary tax farmers known as *zamindars* in Bengal and *talukadars* in Awadh and Hyderabad collected the land tax in exchange for 10 percent of all the funds they raised. Company officials took responsibility for most of their own revenue collection, but in the late eighteenth century they sought to raise India's taxable agricultural output by transforming these tax collectors into a class of hereditary landlords. Individual rent-paying farmers undertook most of the actual cultivation, and the Company encouraged the zamindars to invest in improved agricultural production by giving them formal title to the land they administered. This permanent settlement, as the reforms came to be known, altered substantially the basis of land rights in northeastern India. Most individual farmers became tenants of the zamindars, who now held legal title to their land.

Although this system allowed the Company to collect almost 50 percent of Bengal's gross annual produce in taxes by the beginning of the nineteenth century, the permanent settlement did not live up to expectations. Instead of becoming progressive gentlemanly farmers on the English model, the zamindars behaved more like absentee rent-collecting English landlords in Ireland. Since many Bengalis had difficulty paying their increased taxes, an estimated one-third of the land in Bengal changed hands in the decades immediately following the settlement. Much of it fell into the hands of Calcutta merchants who had tied their fortunes to the Company a century earlier.

CONSOLIDATION AND EXPANSION IN THE IMPERIAL CENTURY

The value of the Bengal land revenues, and to a lesser degree the revenues of Madras and Bombay, made India Britain's most valuable overseas possession at the start of the imperial century. British East India Company bonds paid from 8 to 12 percent per year, and annual revenues, which totaled over £20 million in the first decades of the century, helped balance Britain's trade deficit with China. The Company also transferred a substantial portion of these funds directly to Britain as "home charges" in the form of bullion, administrative salaries, pensions, stock dividends, freight charges, insurance, and banking fees.

Yet in spite of this increasing profitability, the BEIC fought to justify its total control of the Indian economy during the metropolitan backlash against the restrictions of the mercantilist system. When the Company's charter came up for renewal in 1813, free traders managed to abolish its monopoly over Indian trade. The new charter allowed the Company to retain its local monopolies only on salt and opium production. By 1834, the Company's stock ceased to trade, and shareholders received an annual dividend of roughly 10 percent of the total revenues of British India. Thus during the era of informal empire, the British East India Company remade itself into a political institution. The Company's primary focus became administration and revenue collection, even though it remained technically a privately held commercial enterprise.

Although the British government gained a much greater say in Company affairs, company officials in India still enjoyed a considerable degree of autonomy because their lucrative tax base allowed them to remain financially independent. The most effective method of meeting rising administrative costs and making the Company more profitable was to acquire more taxable territory. Therefore the BEIC freely employed its large standing army to expand its borders and subdue its remaining Indian rivals. During the first decades of the imperial century, Company forces vanquished the powerful Hindu Maratha states on the Deccan Plateau, as well as the Sikhs of the Punjab, and occupied extensive territories on India's northwestern and northeastern frontiers.

On other occasions, the Company expanded its influence by administrative fiat rather than force of arms. It decreed that the rulers of the semiautonomous princely states who had acknowledged the suzerainty of the Company by accepting British residents into their courts could not designate an adopted heir if they were childless. Under what became known as the Doctrine of Lapse, the Company inherited the lands and possessions of these princes and rajas when they died. Thus by the mid-nineteenth century the BEIC had completely subjugated the subcontinent. Powerful rulers in the interior like the sultan of Mysore and the nizam of Hyderabad survived as British vassals, while the Company maintained direct control over vast stretches of territory in Bengal, the Northwestern Provinces, and India's coasts.

One of the great ironies of India's imperial era was that the Company's conquest of the subcontinent was carried out largely by Indians. The Indian army made Britain a great land power, but it was essentially an Indian institution led by a handful of British officers and stiffened by a core of British regular soldiers. In 1848, the army consisted of approximately 29,000 Europeans and 235,000 Indian soldiers known as sepoys. Although it may appear incongruous for Indians to have served their foreign conquerors, a large percentage of the Mughals' armies had also been composed of Hindus and other non-Muslims. Company recruiters exploited ethnic, religious, and class divisions among Indians, and there was no greater Indian national identity for these soldiers to betray. Moreover, the Company paid generous salaries, offered pensions for fifteen years of reliable service, and gave its soldiers precedence in civil lawsuits.

The British East India Company relied on Indians at the administrative level as well. Although it fired most of its Indian employees in the late eighteenth century to prevent them from "corrupting" their British co-workers, its civil service never numbered more than approximately 2,000 Europeans. Thus even though the Company abandoned its original commercial function, it still lacked the personnel and resources to govern India directly. This was particularly true in the Indian countryside, since there were rarely more than one or two British officials in a given district. Britain itself did not have a modern police force until 1829, and the Company did not have the manpower or popular support to create a similar organization for India. Instead, it simply absorbed Indian village watchmen and headmen into its local administration. The watchmen, known as *chaukidars* in Bengal, were primarily responsible for suppressing rural banditry. Village headmen interpreted the Company's rules and regulations for the general population and advised British officials on local affairs. Both groups were poorly paid and had little reason to be loyal to the Company. Therefore, they often enriched themselves substantially by accepting bribes and exercising their authority selectively.

Company officials were usually forced to tolerate these practices because they could not afford to meddle too deeply in Indian affairs. They co-opted local legal and bureaucratic institutions to avoid provoking widespread social unrest. The Company adapted the Mughal administrative system to govern most of India and based its law codes on Hindu and Muslim legal texts. The Company also formalized the residency system to exert greater influence in the princely states. British residents manipulated these nominally autonomous rulers by taking informal control of their foreign relations, armed forces, and financial affairs. For the most part, the princes retained their wealth and social status, but the growing influence of the Company's residents in effect reduced them to ceremonial figureheads. This system of indirect rule became the model for British colonial administration in much of Africa.

Although company officials tried to minimize the social disruption caused by their expanding political role, they tried to improve India's productivity by intervening freely in its agrarian and economic affairs. The BEIC derived roughly a quarter of its total income from its monopoly on salt and opium production. Almost 40 percent of its revenue came from land taxes, which amounted to almost £18 million by the mid-nineteenth century. Thus the Company emulated its Mughal predecessors by extracting the agricultural surplus of India.

This reliance on Indian agriculture made company officials particularly concerned with issues relating to taxation and land tenure. The Company surveyed rural India extensively to streamline the Mughal revenue collection system. Land assessments therefore increased substantially at the beginning of the imperial century. Most levies averaged half of the annual value of a farmer's crops, and officials allowed no exemptions for special hardships such as drought or insect infestation. The Company taxed Bengal's zamindar landholders under the terms of the permanent settlement but adopted a substantially different policy in the Bombay and Madras presidencies. Instead of trying to turn tax collectors into landlords, officials in southern and western India encouraged free peasants known as *ryots* to improve their land in order to take advantage of greater access to global markets. Finally, in the Punjab and Northwestern provinces, the Company also encouraged individual land ownership but directed peasants to pay their taxes communally as a village.

The Company generally did not encourage the development of plantation agriculture in India on the Caribbean model. The one exception was in northeastern India, where European planters grew indigo, opium, and tea in Bengal, Bihar, and Assam. Yet even there the planters did not own large estates. Instead, they loaned Indian peasants money to cover their rent to the zamindars, and, in return, the peasants agreed to grow cash crops on a fixed portion of their land. Indian opium growers were relatively well treated because the Company still held a monopoly on opium production, but peasants growing indigo were largely at the mercy of planters who conspired with zamindars and hoodlums to force them into inequitable long-term contracts. This use of excessive force and unfree labor practices embarrassed company officials and threatened to spark serious social unrest. They therefore gradually forced the planters out of business as indigo became less profitable.

The limited success of plantation agriculture in India reaffirmed the British East India Company's reliance on indigenous Indian agriculture. Officials tried to ensure that their agrarian policies did not cause undue social disruption, but the era of Company rule accelerated and distorted profound changes that were already taking place in rural Indian society. A shortage of agricultural labor kept land prices low in the eighteenth century and ensured that there was usually enough land for any farmer who wanted it. Land became more valuable in the nineteenth century as population growth, expanded cash crop production, rising agricultural prices, expanded irrigation, and increased transportation absorbed the remaining reserves of unused land. The Company did not have the capacity to entirely restructure India's rural economy, but it helped make prime agricultural land a salable commodity by fixing individual land tenure to improve taxation.

These changes had a number of unexpected consequences. Indian moneylenders, who had previously used a peasant's crops as collateral, foreclosed on the farms themselves when a peasant went bankrupt.

Company officials feared that these moneylenders were more interested in land speculation than agricultural production but could do little to arrest the process that they themselves had helped set in motion. Instead of reshaping India's rural economy to suit its own ends, the Company simply changed the rules of the game. On the plus side, moneylenders and commodity traders prospered from rising land values and the commercialization of agriculture. Conversely, the old warrior Indian castes that derived status from feudalistic systems of landholding declined, and small farmers often lost their land altogether.

In addition to these economic ramifications, mounting political pressure in Britain forced the Company to relax its policy of noninterference in Indian social affairs as the century progressed. Company officials believed that religion governed all aspects of Indian society and therefore adopted a strict ban on Christian evangelism. In an effort to rule by "Indian tradition," the Company based its legal system on Hindu and Muslim scriptures as interpreted by high-caste Brahmans and senior Islamic scholars. In the late eighteenth century, high-ranking company officials rejected proposals to create an English-based education system in India and instead established the Islamic Calcutta Madrassa and the Hindu Sanskrit College to train young Indians for administrative and legal positions in the Company. To further establish their legitimacy, company officials emulated their Indian predecessors by casting themselves as protectors of local cemeteries, shrines, and temples.

Although these practices helped minimize the social impact of the Company's invasive economic policies, they provoked widespread condemnation from British Evangelicals, who attacked the Company for its tolerance of Indian "barbarism." In the eighteenth century would-be British missionaries worked out of the Dutch enclave of Serampore to escape the Company's prohibition on proselytization. As has already been noted, in the early nineteenth century the Evangelical movement joined with free traders to attack the BEIC's monopolistic control of Indian commerce and society. Led by William Wilberforce, a prominent Evangelical and abolitionist, the Clapham Sect collected over half a million signatures on petitions demanding an end to the Company's toleration of anti-Christian practices in India. These included *sati* (or suttee), the self-immolation of a Hindu widow on her husband's funeral pyre; *thagi,* an itinerant religious sect that murdered hapless travelers; female infanticide; and human sacrifice. Just as the Company lost its commercial monopoly when its charter was renewed in 1813 and 1833, the British government also forced it to abolish restrictions on Christian proselytization in India.

Although older company officials considered these changes to be dangerous, others, influenced by liberal Utilitarian ideals, believed in strengthening British rule by reforming Indian society through free trade, evangelism, Western law, and English education. Many prominent Utilitarians joined the BEIC in the first decades of the nineteenth century as it became less a commercial enterprise and more a governing bureaucracy. Both James Mill and his son John Stuart Mill held clerical and administrative roles in the Company. As advocates of "good government," the Mills and their Utilitarian allies joined Evangelicals in condemning what they perceived to be India's backwardness and moral stagnation. Their cure for India's ills was Western legal reform and the full-scale Anglicization of Indian society.

Unlike their eighteenth-century predecessors, these new company officials had little respect for Indian cultures and traditions. Thomas Babington Macaulay, who was responsible for educational and legal reform, opined that "a single shelf of a good European library was worth the whole native literature of India and Arabia." Moreover, in a drastic shift from earlier Company policy, he argued in 1835 that "we must at present do our best to form a class who may be interpreters between us and the millions whom we govern, a class of persons Indian in blood and colour, but English in taste, in opinions, in morals and intellect."

Macaulay and the Utilitarians sought to create this new Anglicized middle class by transforming Indian education. They created English-based universities in the main presidency towns, which differed from earlier missionary colleges by using English literature rather than the Bible as the basis of instruction. Evangelicals branded the new secular curriculum atheistic, but it allowed Indian students to acquire a Western education without converting to Christianity. The success of the new universities also allowed the Company to replace Persian, the language of the Mughal court, with English as the primary language of Indian administration.

To a limited extent, the English-language universities succeeded in creating an Anglicized Indian middle class. Most of the new graduates were the sons of India's literate classes, who embraced an English education as means of social advancement in British India. The Charter Act of

1833 specifically barred the Company from practicing racial discrimination, and the new graduates filled the lower ranks of its civil service. With their own English-language newspapers and commitment to social reform, they were a dynamic force in Indian society. Most were Hindus, since Muslims found it more difficult to accommodate themselves to Western education, no matter how secular the new universities appeared to be. Dwarkanath Tagore was the first Indian to hold a high position in the Company. A prominent zamindar, he served on the Company's board of customs, founded India's first Western-style bank, and was a leading investor in Indian-owned coal mines and steamship lines. Ram Mohan Roy, another leading Hindu intellectual, became the assistant to the collector of Rangpur and served as the Mughal emperor's representative in London.

Although many students embraced Western education and commerce as a means of modernizing India, it would be a mistake to see them as "English in taste, in opinions, in morals and intellect." Even though students of the Young Bengal Movement threw beef into the houses of leading Calcutta Brahmans to protest the restrictions of conservative Hinduism, they did not divorce themselves completely from their cultural roots. To many Western-educated Hindus, British education and culture offered the means to reform and strengthen Indian society. The Hindu reformers were opposed by conservative scholars, many of whom interpreted Hindu law for the Company and maintained a vested interest in emphasizing the authoritative role of religious texts and scriptures in Indian society.

Many of the practices that India's British critics labeled barbaric were at the center of these debates. When Ram Mohan Roy supported the Company's 1829 ban on sati, he argued the practice of widow burning was not an organic part of Hinduism. Rather, he maintained that sati was primarily an innovation of high-caste Hindu priests who wanted to discipline potentially unfaithful wives. Although Indian conservatives argued that reformers had misread and ignored key passages from Hindu scriptures, the Company's tabulation of widow-burning incidents in the years preceding its ban supported Roy's position. Sati appears to have been rarely practiced among the greater Hindu population in the early nineteenth century, but over 60 percent of the 8,124 recorded incidents of sati in 1829 involved upper-caste Hindus living in Calcutta.

Thus British rule created a new environment for interpreting, contesting, and even inventing Indian "traditions." Both conservative religious elites and westernized reformers sought to exploit the restrictions and opportunities presented by the growing commercialization of Indian society under foreign rule by defining tradition. The British administration was only dimly aware of this debate, and the success or failure of the competing factions was based largely on their ability to convince British officials of the authenticity of a particular interpretation of Indian tradition. Thus the introduction of Western education did not modernize Indian society as British reformers had intended. Instead, an English-style education provided the new commercial elites with the means to challenge the dominant position of the older, often feudalistic classes in Indian society.

INDIA UNDER THE BRITISH RAJ

Although elements of India's educated and commercial classes successfully exploited the opportunities presented by the new imperial order, the tacit acquiescence of the general populace that enabled a handful of British officials to govern the Indian majority was, in turn, undermined by the significant social and economic tensions that a century of Company rule had produced. These pressures came to a head in April 1857, exactly one hundred years after the Battle of Plassey, when three regiments of the Bengal army stationed at Meerut near Delhi executed their British officers and proclaimed the restoration of the Mughal emperor. The sepoys had numerous grievances, but the immediate cause of the mutiny was a rumor that cartridges for the newly introduced Enfield rifle were greased with a mixture of pork and beef fat. If the stories had been true, the cartridges would have contaminated any devout Hindu or Muslim soldier who used them.

In the past, sepoys had struck occasionally to protest a variety of issues relating to religion, uniforms, and foreign service, but the 1857 mutiny was unique in its scope and severity. The soldiers' open defiance of British authority weakened the coercive bonds that kept the general Indian population in check. The military insurrection grew swiftly into a general civil revolt in the Northwestern provinces, the Maratha states, and western Bengal. The most affected areas were key recruiting centers and regions that had experienced a high degree of social and economic dislocation under British rule. Yet there was little to bind the rebels together other than an intense dissatisfaction with company rule. Many landowners, squeezed by high tax rates, lost their holdings to money-lenders. Peasants and nomadic peoples also resented their loss of access to communal grazing lands, and the few Indian princes who joined the revolt saw the Doctrine of Lapse as a barely disguised excuse to annex their domains. These multiple grievances make it difficult to categorize the mutiny definitively, and modern historians have labeled it variously a rural revolt, a Muslim holy war, a Mughal restoration, a Hindu Maratha revival, and an Indian national movement.

Britain contained the rebellion because it was limited largely to the Bengal presidency. For the most part, southern and western India remained quiet, and educated Indians and most of the semiautonomous rulers of princely states also remained largely uninvolved. Nevertheless, the mutiny remains one of the most bloody and expensive episodes in the history of British India. In one sense, it resembled a civil war because the rebels and mutineers turned on members of India's newly Anglicized educated and commercial classes. British officials, however, were more alarmed by violent Indian attacks on the general British population. The rebels refused to spare European women and children, and the British press popularized lurid but untrue stories that female victims were raped before they were killed.

These incidents made the British acutely aware of their physical and strategic vulnerability. With only 45,000 European soldiers in all of India, the Company relied heavily on newly recruited Sikh soldiers, loyal Bengali sepoys, and the Madras and Bombay armies during the fourteen-month-long campaign to reconquer the rebellious north. When the British were ultimately victorious, individual officers sought retribution for the lurid atrocities sensationalized in the popular press. Their revenge, predicated on the assumption that religion ruled Indian society, was intended to defile the mutineers. The victors forced Muslims to eat pork before they were cremated and Hindus to eat beef before they were buried. These wholesale executions were as barbarous as any of the outrages perpetrated by the rebels, and they undermined the paternalistic ideology that legitimized British rule in India. All told, the mutiny cost Britain £50 million and over 11,000 British soldiers, lost to both fighting and disease. There are no reliable figures for rebel losses, but historians estimate that, at the very least, hundreds of thousands of

Indian soldiers and civilians died as a result of the fighting and British reprisals.

The psychological and economic cost of the mutiny forced British officials to reevaluate the basic philosophical tenets by which they had governed India during the first half of the imperial century. Prime Minister Benjamin Disraeli told the House of Commons in 1857 that the unrest was due to a conservative backlash against British social engineering. British officials had hoped to win the support of the common Indian through good government and rural prosperity, and they were shocked when such a large segment of the peasantry of central and northeastern India rose against them. Evangelicals and Utilitarians of the 1830s and 1840s believed that they could restructure Indian society, but after 1857 most officials concluded that in general Indians were too superstitious and fanatical to assimilate Western cultural values.

It is now clear, however, that the mutiny was not a backlash against modernity. The epicenter of the revolt in the Northwestern provinces, central India, and the princely state of Awadh had experienced British rule for only a few decades. Calcutta and most of Bengal, which had been governed by the Company for an entire century, experienced little unrest during the mutiny. Moreover, it is hard to attribute the initial sepoy insurrection at Meerut to religious fanaticism, since the same Hindu and Muslim soldiers willingly used the offending cartridges against the British. In the final analysis, the mutiny was simply the spark that ignited simmering discontent over fundamental social and economic changes brought on by British rule. Britain weathered the storm because only a few areas experienced the full effects of its most invasive policies and because a substantial segment of India's commercial classes, educated elites, and princely rulers exploited successfully the opportunities presented by British imperial rule.

Nevertheless, the mutiny convinced British officials in London that they needed to take a more direct hand in governing their most important imperial possession. The era of Company rule in India finally came to an end when the last of the rebels were defeated. In 1858, Parliament passed the Act for the Better Government of India, which established the India Office as a formal branch of the British government. It was responsible to the secretary of state for India. He presided over a council of fifteen advisers who replaced the Company's old board of control.

In India, the abolition of the company eliminated the usefulness of the Mughal emperor as a legitimizing figurehead, and the elderly Bahadur Shah was tried for treason and exiled. Disraeli designated Queen Victoria "Empress of India," and India's new imperial government became known as the Raj. The governor-general of Bengal thereby became the British monarch's viceroy. To keep him better apprised of public opinion, the Indian Councils' Act of 1861 provided for nominal Indian representation, largely in an advisory capacity, on legislative councils in the three main presidency towns. The Indian civil service, which became Britain's premier imperial bureaucracy under the Raj, remained responsible for basic administrative functions. A competitive examination system instituted in 1853 opened the civil service to talent, and high salaries and generous pensions attracted some of the most capable members of the British middle class.

British officials also restructured the Indian army to forestall future mutinies. To keep the most potent instruments of war in British hands, they disbanded all Indian artillery units. They discharged all regular European soldiers and garrisoned India with battalions of the regular British army. British officials also altered the ethnic composition of the Indian army dramatically. The traumatic recollection of rebellious Indian troops murdering British officers shook their confidence in all non-European soldiers. Even though many Bengali sepoys had refused to join the mutineers, senior British military officials concluded that the security and prosperity of British rule had made the men of Bengal too selfish and "effeminate" to be reliable soldiers. In practical terms, they recruited sepoys from regions that had yet to experience the full impact of the economic and social dislocations produced by imperial rule. British recruiting officers restocked the Indian army with Nepalese Gurkhas, Sikhs, and Punjabi Muslims. The Raj also bestowed substantial irrigation projects on the latter two regions to reduce the chance that sepoy grievances over its agrarian policies might spark further unrest.

British officials sought to further apply the apparent lessons of the mutiny by making the new Raj more responsive to conservative forces in Indian society. The reformers abandoned the Utilitarians' Anglicization experiment, placed new restrictions on Christian evangelism, and sought to co-opt and reinforce Indian customs and traditions. The Raj had little use for the Indian educated and commercial classes, which had failed to convince the general population of the value of British rule. British officials instead sought to increase their legitimacy by allying themselves with the forces of "tradition" in the countryside. Assuming that the mutiny was partially a response to land foreclosures by grasping moneylenders, they tried to appease both landlords and peasants by decreasing the land tax.

Lord Charles Canning, the first British viceroy, rewarded Indian princes who had remained loyal during the revolt by ending the Doctrine of Lapse. Depicting the Raj as a great Indian power, he invented a set of new imperial Indian "traditions" to legitimize British rule. Canning created the Star of India and the Order of Indian Empire for loyal princes and senior British officials, and he awarded cooperative rulers with the titles Raja, Nawab, Rai, and Bahadur. The government's Alqabnamah Register listed the formal titles and privileges of every prince, including his coat of arms, the number of guns in his official salute, and the color of the crest on his official correspondence. The British viceroys staged grand public displays known as Durbars to celebrate and nurture these new imperial institutions. The resulting official culture of the Raj was therefore neither exclusively British nor Indian. Rather, it was a cultural hybrid that adapted and invented Indian institutions to legitimize British rule.

The sweeping political and social reforms that gave rise to the Raj were also a product of the changing economic basis of British imperialism in India. The mutiny took place at a time when British leaders were losing faith in free trade and informal empire in the face of aggressive competition from European rivals. They therefore began to look upon India primarily as a reserved market for British trade and investment rather than as a source of raw materials or land revenues. Although these changes were already under way before 1857, the mutiny accelerated the shift by demonstrating the danger of excessive land taxes and the inefficiency of the British East India Company. British officials realized that efforts to increase land revenues by stimulating Indian agricultural production were socially disruptive and that license fees, income taxes, and customs duties were safer sources of revenue.

India's economic relationship with Britain under the Raj could not be termed mercantilistic because foreigners had access to Indian markets, but imperial rule ensured that the Indian economy was structured to favor British interests. In the late nineteenth century, Britain financed almost two-thirds of its growing international trade deficit with Indian exports of jute, cotton, and tea to Europe, and rice and opium to the Far

East. Furthermore, roughly 85 percent of India's imports in the 1880s and 1890s came from Britain, which amounted to almost 20 percent of all British foreign exports during the period. Most of these British imports consisted of cotton textiles, hardware, iron, and steel. Britain's spinning and weaving industries, which had great difficulty keeping up with their more modern European competitors, were particularly dependent on Indian markets. By 1913, over 40 percent of all British textile exports went to India. Lancashire manufacturers were acutely aware of this dependence and used their influence in the British Liberal Party to block an attempt by the Raj to raise revenue by increasing Indian tariffs.

Yet India was more than just a prop for Britain's increasingly outmoded and inefficient industrial sector. Its greatest value to Britain at the end of the imperial century was as a lucrative outlet for British capital. From 1865 to 1914, London financiers invested over £2.5 million in India, which made the Raj the second most favored investment in the British Empire, after Canada. The great majority of this capital went into developing the Indian railway network, which encompassed 34,000 miles of track in 1913. British administrators backed railway construction for a number of reasons. The rail system made the Raj more secure by allowing the small garrison of British troops to deal swiftly with civil unrest. Moreover, railways gave British manufacturers greater access to Indian markets and helped Indian farmers sell their produce abroad.

Although the railway stimulated the Indian economy, its construction was a windfall to British manufacturers and investors. Most of its infrastructure was imported from Britain, and highly paid British workers supplied most of the skilled labor on the project. The Raj raised the enormous sums of money needed to build this vast subcontinental rail system by guaranteeing investors profits of at least 4.5 percent. It therefore had to borrow funds at high rates of interest to make good on this commitment whenever the railways failed to return a sufficient profit. The burden of these railway subsidies, coupled with the cost of the Indian army and other administrative obligations, inflated the Indian national debt substantially. India's total obligations to its creditors amounted to almost half the value of its total exports in the later half of the nineteenth century, and by 1900 the interest alone on this debt amounted to £10 million per year.

Many Indian intellectuals resented this forced indebtedness and charged that British rule retarded India's development by siphoning off funds that the country needed to industrialize. This view was actually first advanced by a former British revenue commissioner for Bombay in 1859; it was subsequently popularized by Romesh Chandar Dutt, a one-time lecturer at the University of London and president of the Indian National Congress. Proponents of this theory of "drain" pointed to the British East India Company's commercial monopoly, excessive land taxes, and unreasonably low tariffs favoring Lancashire textile interests as evidence of India's subordinate economic relationship with Britain. They argued Indian taxpayers were unfairly saddled with responsibility for the "home charges," which included the annual cost of interest on the national debt, government contracts that were filled in Britain, administrative costs for both the Raj and the London-based India Office, and pensions for retired British officials. Dutt and his allies also complained that the unreasonably large and expensive Indian army absorbed almost 40 percent of the national budget. Not only did Indian taxpayers have to maintain the British garrison in India, but they also had to pay for any foreign campaign involving Indian troops that the British government deemed to be in the general interest of India. As costly as these obligations may have been, however, it is still not certain that they hindered India's industrial development. Indians certainly subsidized the British Empire, but modern historians have calculated that the home charges constituted only a tiny fraction of India's gross national income.

Nevertheless, it is clear that Britain's dependence on India grew considerably in the closing decades of the imperial century. The defense and security of the Raj clearly preoccupied British officials in London during the era of the "new" imperialism. In terms of foreign policy, the British government was obsessed with protecting India's borders and links with the rest of the empire. At the domestic level, traumatic memories of 1857 made British administrators acutely concerned with the stability of Indian society. Yet their attempts to co-opt the forces of "tradition" actually accelerated the social and economic transformation of India under British rule.

INDIA AT THE END OF THE IMPERIAL CENTURY

The Indian mutiny taught British imperialists the risks of trying to govern non-Western societies by remaking them in their own image.

Believing that they had become dangerously detached from the general population, British administrators worked to reestablish their legitimacy in the eyes of what they perceived to be India's most influential classes. In practical terms, they sought to co-opt at least a segment of Indian society by demonstrating the value of participating in the imperial system. Prior to 1857, a Western-style education was the key to taking advantage of these opportunities, but the most influential Indians under the Raj were those who successfully depicted themselves at the arbiters of Indian "tradition." Although many Indians suffered considerably from economic and social dislocations during the imperial century, the imperial system had the capacity to enrich groups and individuals who could successfully exploit the possibilities inherent in British rule.

In the countryside, the Raj offered significant opportunities to Indian farmers through increased access to world markets via the railway and the development of an extensive irrigation system. The network of canals in the northern Indian province of Uttar Pradesh watered 2.5 million acres of land in times of drought. Although overirrigation waterlogged low-lying lands and reduced soil fertility in others by raising saline levels, the steady and reliable supply of water enriched efficient Indian farmers by allowing them to switch from subsistence food production to cash crops.

Yet the potential benefits of the Raj's railways and canals were tempered by British attempts to stimulate agricultural production and facilitate tax collection by shifting landholding in rural India from customary communal rights to individual ownership. In other words, British rule offered the prize of private land tenure to farmers and landlords who could afford to pay their taxes. In northern India, British officials gave Rajput elites title to 60 percent of Banda district at the beginning of the era of company rule. By 1874, however, these elites had lost 30 percent of their holdings to foreclosure and public auction. Much of the district was subsequently acquired by Muslim commercial families who used their administrative connections to purchase the land at reduced prices.

In the south, the Raj's insistence that land taxes had to be paid in cash often forced ryots (peasant farmers) to mortgage their land to wealthy rural elites when their crops failed. These rural magnates were far better equipped to exploit the possibilities of the imperial system by producing cash crops for the world market. Many bought up the harvests of individual ryots and made more money as commodity speculators than as actual farmers. Small producers who lost their land were faced with the choice of becoming sharecroppers or moving to the cities to look for paid employment. To be sure, these changes were due in part to population pressure and a worldwide demand for Indian produce, but the Raj's agricultural policies clearly accelerated the process by helping to make rural land a salable commodity.

British rule also created similar opportunities and pitfalls in the commercial and industrial fields. In the 1850s Karl Marx expected British imperialism to industrialize India by sweeping away "feudal" elements in Indian society. Yet the introduction of low-cost, mass-produced British cotton goods bankrupted India's indigenous textile sector. Although other handicraft industries devoted to leather, metal, and woodworking survived, all but a few wealthy Indians preferred moneylending and petty trading to manufacturing. Moreover, India's loss of sovereignty deprived would-be Indian manufacturers of the protective tariffs that allowed their European counterparts to defend developing industries from foreign competition. British manufacturing interests often used their political influence to hinder the development of rival Indian enterprises, and officials in London discouraged the Raj from purchasing Indian products. The Indian government could purchase locally produced Indian iron only if it cost at least 5 percent less than imported British iron.

Despite these restrictions, a small Indian industrial sector developed by taking advantage of the opportunities that British rule offered. India had ample supplies of coal, and the displacement of peasant farmers in the countryside created a relatively inexpensive wage labor force. Railways provided ready access to both Indian and world markets, and Indian manufacturers profited from Britain's commitment to free trade. As a result, hostile Lancashire magnates could not prevent India from becoming the world's fourth largest cotton manufacturer on the eve of the First World War. Successful Indian entrepreneurs often used textiles as a launching pad for other ventures. J. N. Tata, who made his fortune in Bombay cotton, founded India's first indigenous steel industry in 1907 after an influx of cheap European imports forced the Raj to abandon its restrictions on Indian industrial development. When British bankers refused to help him raise capital, he sold over £1.5 million in shares to individual Indian investors. Although British rule limited India's industrial development substantially, it did provide the means and opportunity for a small handful of entrepreneurs to lay the groundwork for an indigenous manufacturing sector.

Furthermore, the British imperial system had profound social, as well as economic, ramifications. British officials tended to base their administrative policies on the assumption that Indian society was defined and ordered by tribe, caste, and religion. With a limited understanding of Indian social practices, these officials relied primarily on orthodox Hindu and Muslim texts to interpret these categories. Yet Indian identities were far more complex and fluid than the British realized. The designation tribe had no cultural or national meaning, and it was usually applied to the seminomadic, clan-based societies on the frontiers of agrarian India. These peoples could transform themselves into Muslims or Hindus simply by adopting a more settled lifestyle. Moreover, the most influential Hindu scriptures describe four principle castes: Brahman (priest), Kshatriya (warrior), Vaishya (trader), and Sudra (farmer or artisan). In addition to a category of social outcasts known as the untouchables, however, there were over 3,000 subcastes based largely on occupation. Whereas British officials believed that Hindu castes were primordial and unchanging, there is substantial evidence of considerable intermarriage between the various subcastes before the nineteenth century. Similarly, the debate over sati has demonstrated conflicting interpretations of what constituted religious orthodoxy. Thus, as in most other parts of the world, Indians conceptualized identity in response to specific political, economic, and social tensions. It is therefore not surprising that they often shifted or transformed their identities as these realities changed over time.

British rule made this relatively fluid system far more rigid. By favoring scripture over customary law, British officials encouraged the development of more rigid and legalistic conceptions of Hinduism and Islam, which tended to fix religion as a social category. Furthermore, the British helped make tribal and caste-based identities more inelastic by setting "tradition" as the basis of political and social legitimacy. Groups and individuals that successfully depicted themselves as "traditional" leaders of their particular communities were in the best position to manipulate the imperial system. To cite a few examples, after the mutiny, recruiters restricted the lucrative occupation of military service to the "martial races" of India on the assumption that certain Indian tribes and castes were "naturally" suited to be loyal soldiers. Similarly, British officials tried to limit the influence of moneylenders in northwestern India by passing the Punjab Land Alienation Act of 1900, which decreed that only members of "agricultural tribes" could purchase land.

On the other hand, groups that had their identities fixed for them by outsiders often suffered under the Raj. The Criminal Tribes Act of 1871 empowered the Indian government to name any "tribe, gang or class of persons" a "criminal tribe." This statute gave the government the authority to confine such groups to a fixed area and to discipline any who resisted with fines, corporal punishment, and imprisonment. Although British officials believed that caste (and even biology) made these groups "natural" criminals, in reality most of the "criminal tribes" were like the Banjaras, a subcaste of transportation specialists who took to banditry after the Indian rail system destroyed their livelihood.

The Raj's efforts to use identity to control unrest demonstrate clearly that Indians did not react passively to British social and economic meddling. Although the imperial system offered substantial opportunity to a fortunate few, on the whole it was a confining garment that fitted the general Indian population far too tightly. The 1857 mutiny demonstrated the folly of contesting British authority with armed force, but Indians did use their force of numbers to resist the social and economic transformation of India under British rule.

This was particularly the case in rural areas, as lower-class field laborers, herdsmen, and even village watchmen regularly turned to banditry in times of economic hardship. Lacking the arms and organization to attack the British administration directly, they terrorized landlords and moneylenders who prospered under the imperial system. British officials attributed these incidents to the "primitive superstitions" of rural India, but in reality they were a potent form of social protest. Unlike the British East India Company, the Raj had a small European police force, but its policemen still had to rely on village watchmen and headmen to assert their authority throughout the vast countryside. As a small and isolated ruling minority, British officials lacked the capacity to discipline the lower levels of Indian society.

By the late nineteenth century, Indian peasants learned to exploit this weakness by organizing mass protests against unpopular government policies. During the 1896 famine on the Deccan Plateau, large numbers of small landholders simply refused to pay their taxes. With the trauma of the 1857 mutiny never far from their minds, British officials were reluctant to push the Indian peasantry too far. They therefore tempered their support for the Indian landlord class with legislation designed to offer peasant farmers a measure of protection from the dislocation caused by British efforts to restructure the rural economy. The Rent Act of 1859 granted long-term occupancy rights to sharecroppers who worked a plot of land for more than twelve years, and it limited a landlord's right to confiscate the crops of delinquent tenants. The Deccan Agriculturalists Relief Act of 1879 placed a ceiling on peasant debts and restricted land transfers in order to give moneylenders less of an incentive to foreclose on delinquent farmers.

Although these reforms were generally successful in preventing outbreaks of serious rural unrest, the most potent Indian challenge to the legitimacy of the Raj came not from the countryside but from the cities. India's commercial and educated classes rejected their diminished status after the mutiny and became increasingly impatient with the discriminatory aspects of the imperial system as the nineteenth century drew to a close. Graduates of India's Western-style universities had few suitable career prospects beyond the limited scope of medicine, law, journalism, or education. They were barred from the upper levels of the government and the military, and the business and manufacturing sectors were dominated by British interests. To make matters worse, the British popular press ridiculed educated Indians as pretentious and semicivilized "babus." Most educated elites remained committed to "modernizing" India along Western lines in spite of this abuse and discrimination, but after 1857 they began to conclude that they could do so without the aid of Britain.

In 1885 educated Hindus in Bombay founded the Indian National Congress with the assistance of a retired British administrator. The viceroy had hoped the organization would confine itself to providing advice on social issues, but its members used the Congress to publicize their grievances with the Raj. Members called for lower land taxes, a reduction in the Indian army, and greater investment in Indian agriculture, industry, and education. In the administrative field, they wanted civil service exams held in India rather than London and insisted on the right of the Raj's Indian judges to hear cases concerning Europeans. Before the First World War few Congress members called for an independent India; most hoped to capture the Raj by opening its bureaucratic and political institutions to qualified Indians.

British officials tried to appease the nationalists through gradual constitutional concessions. The Indian Councils Act of 1892 granted Indians increased representation on both central and provincial legislative councils. When the Indian National Congress grew more influential after the turn of the century, the Morley-Minto Reforms of 1909 increased Indian representation yet again, allowing directly elected Indian legislators to propose resolutions and initiate debate on legislative matters. The Raj sought to isolate the most radical nationalists by giving moderate Indians a stake in the imperial system but had limited success because it refused to surrender its monopoly on Indian politics. In spite of the reforms, British officials retained a majority on all legislative councils and diluted the influence of the Hindu majority by reserving a specific number of seats for Muslims.

British rule would certainly have become untenable had the Indian National Congress been able to acquire a broad popular following, but its influence was limited by the religious and social background of its members. To be sure, prominent Congressmen mobilized large segments of Hindu society to protest unpopular government policies. Surendranath Banerjea challenged the privileged status accorded British economic interests by founding the *swadeshi* ("of our own country") movement, which organized a successful mass boycott of British products. Yet the Congress had difficulty forming ties with the Indian peasantry because many Congressmen were products of the moneylending classes. These individuals opposed legislation to improve tenant rights and blamed rural unrest on the "drain" of Indian wealth to Britain.

More significantly, many Muslims considered the Congress a predominately Hindu body. A radical faction of Congressmen led by Bal Gangadhar Tilak, a prominent Brahman attorney, openly called for a Hindu revival based on a romanticized image of India in the "golden age" before Muslim rule. The revivalists founded the "cow protection" movement to oppose the slaughter and consumption of Hinduism's most revered animal, and riots broke out in many cities when Hindus tried to block the slaughter of cattle during Islamic holy days. These incidents led prominent Muslims like Sir Sayyid Ahmad Khan to conclude that they might need the Raj as protection from the Hindu majority. Moderate Congress members responded that these fears were unfounded and accused British officials of intentionally fostering communal unrest to divide the Indian nationalist movement.

Mounting Hindu-Muslim tensions at the close of the imperial century were a prelude to the bloody communal strife that would tear India apart at independence in 1947. Although British officials certainly exploited class, caste, religious, and tribal divisions to prevent the Indians from uniting against them, they did not set out to make India ungovernable by turning these identities into rigid and antagonistic social categories. Most Britons in India were only dimly aware of this phenomenon. India's Hindu-Muslim tensions predated British rule, but the intensification of communal antagonism in India during the imperial century was primarily an unforeseen consequence of the administrative tactics that the small cadre of British officials developed to govern the Indian majority. These tactics were so effective that Britain exported them to Africa, and in doing so, saddled their African subjects with many of the same problems that confronted Indians.

SUGGESTIONS FOR FURTHER READING

Ballhatchet, Kenneth. *Race, Sex, and Class under the Raj.* New York: St. Martin's, 1980.

Bayly, C. A. *Indian Society and the Making of the British Empire.* New York: Cambridge University Press, 1990.

Charlesworth, Neil. *British Rule and the Indian Economy, 1800–1914.* London: Macmillan, 1982.

Guha, Ranajit, and C. C. Spivak, eds. *Selected Subaltern Studies.* New York: Oxford University Press, 1988.

Mani, Lata. "Contentious Traditions: The Debate on Sati in Colonial India." In *Recasting Women.* Edited by K. Sangari and S. Vaid. New Brunswick, N.J.: Rutgers University Press, 1990.

Metcalf, Thomas. *Ideologies of the Raj.* Cambridge: Cambridge University Press, 1994.

Robb, Peter, ed. *Rural India.* Delhi: Oxford University Press, 1992.

Spear, Percival. *A History of India.* Vol. 2. New York: Penguin, 1981.

Stokes, Eric. *The Peasant Armed: The Indian Revolt of 1857.* Oxford: Clarendon, 1986.

4

AFRICA

One of the greatest paradoxes of the imperial century was Britain's seemingly inexplicable acquisition of extensive tracts of marginally valuable territory in Africa. Whereas India made substantial contributions of wealth and manpower to the British Empire, few of the new African colonies paid immediate dividends, with the exception of South Africa and Egypt. India had value because the Mughal Empire's extensive bureaucracy had already organized the trade and administration of most of the subcontinent. The British East India Company merely had to co-opt this system to tap India's wealth. Much of Africa, however, was divided into countless small kingdoms and stateless societies whose social and economic institutions could not be as easily captured or restructured by British imperialists. There were no lucrative land taxes to be collected in Africa because many of these societies were organized around communal systems of tenure. In most cases, they had a surplus of land and a shortage of labor, which made it difficult to adapt Indian economic policies to Africa.

Britain had trading contacts with West African coastal states dating back to the sixteenth century, but the few chartered companies operating in the region never remotely approached the success of the British East India Company. Britain did not acquire extensive colonies in Africa until the later third of the imperial century, when it reached a sufficiently advanced state of financial and industrial development to intervene more effectively in African economic and social affairs. The factors that led the British government to abandon its commitment to informal empire are discussed in detail in chapter 1. This chapter explores the impact of the "new" imperialism on Britain's African subjects. For most, the loss of sovereignty during the European "scramble" for the continent was extremely traumatic, and the attempts of British imperialists to make their African colonies more profitable often had tragic results. Yet with extremely limited revenue bases, the new colonial administrations did not have the capacity to govern directly. British officials therefore adapted the Indian system of indirect rule to Africa. Thus in Africa, as in India, certain groups and individuals could lessen the disruptive aspects of imperialism by exploiting the vulnerability of the chronically undermanned and underfunded colonial governments.

AFRICA BEFORE THE PARTITION

One of the main reasons the imperial powers had little difficulty partitioning Africa in the 1880s was that few Africans realized the full implications of the industrial changes taking place in Europe during the imperial century. European contacts with Africa date back to the maritime revolution of the late fifteenth century, when the Portuguese established coastal commercial enclaves throughout the continent. Their attempts to replicate the success of the Spanish conquistadors in the Americas were largely unsuccessful because most African societies were able to defend themselves adequately. Although Dutch settlers known as Afrikaners established a permanent colony on the southern tip of Africa in the 1600s, generally speaking, Europeans trading with Africa before the nineteenth century had to do so on African terms. Moreover, the robust African disease environment kept most foreigners confined to the coasts of tropical Africa, and few peoples living in the interior of the continent had direct contact with Europeans.

British merchants generally concentrated on West Africa before the imperial century. Lacking governmental support, they needed the consent of local rulers to trade for gold, ivory, animal skins, spices, and slaves. African states made considerable profits by monopolizing the production and transportation of these commodities. When Scottish explorer Mungo Park visited the Gambia River in the 1790s, he found the king of Barra charging foreign merchants an entrance duty of £20 per ship to gain admission to the river. Without military backing or protection from endemic contagious diseases, British traders had little choice but to pay local rulers substantial bribes, rents, and tariffs to gain access to West African markets. Africans therefore had little reason to view the

British and their European contemporaries as anything more than profitable trading partners.

The Napoleonic Wars and the British abolitionist movement marked the first substantial changes in the relationship between Europe and Africa. Britain occupied the Dutch colony in southern Africa temporarily after the French invaded the Netherlands in 1795. The increasing value of British India made the naval base at Cape Town a strategically important way station. Britain therefore annexed the Cape Colony as a permanent possession during the Congress of Vienna in 1814 and sought to strengthen its hold on the territory by encouraging increased British settlement to diminish the influence of the Afrikaner inhabitants. In 1835 the Afrikaners responded by making the Great Trek inland and in doing so defeated or displaced the Khoisan- and Bantu-speaking populations of central and eastern South Africa.

In West Africa, the British government had to intervene more directly in African affairs to enforce its 1807 ban on the export of slaves from territories north of the equator. The political influence of the domestic abolitionist lobby made the elimination of slavery a fundamental goal of British foreign policy. Britain used its influence at the Congress of Vienna to force the European maritime nations to sign treaties banning slave trading. The British government tried to reduce the demand for African slaves by compensating West Indian planters for the loss of their human property but did not offer African exporters a comparable substitute for the slave trade. As a result, most African societies refused to recognize Britain's right to regulate their commerce, thereby earning the moral condemnation of the abolitionists. Thus the abolitionist movement shifted the responsibility for the inhuman transatlantic commerce in human beings from the western nations that reaped the benefits of cheap African labor to the Africans themselves.

The British government gave some teeth to the antislavery treaties by using the Royal Navy to stop and search the vessels of suspected smugglers. The West African Anti-Slavery Squadron at one time constituted a sixth of Britain's total naval force and cost as much as £750,000 per year. Yet historians have estimated that the squadron interdicted only 8 percent of the total Atlantic slave trade. The Royal Navy's deep-keeled sailing ships had difficulty operating in the shallow estuaries of the West African coast. Abolitionists therefore pressured the British government to stem the slave trade at its source. Depicting slavery as an African problem, they created a humanitarian excuse to intervene in African affairs. Britain annexed a handful of strategic ports to provide bases for the Royal Navy and offered generous subsidies to local rulers willing to sign antislaving treaties. Those who refused faced the prospect of punitive raids by the Royal Marines.

Britain formally abolished slavery throughout its empire in 1833, but it remained legal in the United States until the 1860s and in Brazil until the 1880s. Few of the European nations that Britain coerced into signing antislavery treaties put much effort into enforcing them, and the abolitionists' moral arguments against slavery carried no weight with European slave traders and African exporters. As a result, Britain had little success in reducing the overall volume of slave exports from Africa in the early decades of the imperial century. Moreover, British attempts to choke off the West African slave trade simply shifted it to other parts of Africa.

Portuguese slave traders, who controlled most of the trans-Atlantic slave traffic in the mid-nineteenth century, exploited a loophole in the antislaving treaties that allowed them to continue to operate south of the equator. They exported approximately 300,000 slaves from Portuguese East Africa (Mozambique) to Brazil, Cuba, and the sugar-producing islands in the Indian Ocean in the 1830s and 1840s. Furthermore, Arab merchants continued to supply Middle Eastern markets with large numbers of East African slaves. Britain's antislavery patrols in the Indian Ocean rarely amounted to more than a handful of small ships; ultimately, slave exports from East Africa actually increased after British intervention in the early nineteenth century.

The relative ineffectiveness of the antislavery squadrons led British abolitionists to conclude that the key to eliminating the slave trade in Africa was to provide Africans with suitable economic alternatives to trafficking in slaves. In *The African Slave Trade and Its Remedy,* published in 1840, leading abolitionist Thomas Buxton argued that Christianity and increased trade were the keys to suppressing African slavery. Although Buxton was sincere in his motives, the abolitionist campaign to convince Africans to embrace "legitimate commerce" also worked to Britain's economic advantage. Reflecting the close ties between British evangelical and commercial interests, Buxton and his allies called on their government to encourage Africans to produce inexpensive exports of cotton, cocoa, palm oil, peanuts, and cloves for British consumption.

Furthermore, British manufacturers hoped to tap new African markets by producing cheap industrial wares to barter for these commodities.

Many Africans willingly embraced legitimate commerce as global prices for tropical raw materials increased over the course of the imperial century. The total value of Britain's palm oil imports alone amounted to almost £1.5 million in the 1860s. Nevertheless, legitimate commerce did not reduce slavery as much as the abolitionists had hoped. In the first place, many successful African planters had never been involved in the slave trade. Moreover, although the gradual abolition of slavery in the Americas eventually weakened powerful African slave-exporting societies, the closure of foreign slave markets simply produced a glut of slaves in Africa. The resulting drop in local slave prices encouraged some African entrepreneurs to rely on slave labor to produce commodities for export.

Furthermore, the growing European demand for African products actually stimulated the expansion of the East African slave trade by encouraging African and Arab ivory hunters to push further into the interior of the continent in search of dwindling elephant herds. Ivory was not an industrial raw material, but the demand for combs, piano keys, billiard balls, and other consumer goods among the growing middle classes of Europe and North America could only be met by the wholesale slaughter of African elephants with modern firearms. This "hunting frontier" sparked political instability and epidemics by introducing guns and infectious disease into previously isolated societies of the East African hinterland.

These peoples were particularly vulnerable to smallpox and other endemic European diseases because they had few direct links to the wider world. Moreover, African hunters often used their guns to prey upon militarily vulnerable societies. They had little difficulty enslaving the survivors of these catastrophic wars and epidemics, and slave caravans carried most of their ivory to the East African coast. Horrified by this increased slave traffic, famous evangelist and explorer David Livingstone concluded that it was a product of Arab greed and African barbarism. He did not understand that it was actually an unforeseen consequence of growing European consumerism.

Yet the social and political consequences of legitimate commerce were not entirely negative. Many African societies exploited successfully the increasing international appetite for tropical raw materials. The palm oil trade in the West African Niger Delta enriched a new class of influential African traders who used their wealth and their access to firearms to create new states. Furthermore, the new trade often empowered those enterprising African women who played a pivotal role in the production and marketing of the new commodities. These developments demonstrate the inaccuracy of the widely held European assumption that African societies were static and unchanging. Whereas much of the African interior was still isolated from the changes taking place in Europe and the Americas, Africans with access to international markets often took advantage of the opportunities presented by the global process of industrialization.

Inspired by the rising value of African markets and raw materials, British imperialists sought firsthand knowledge of the continent in order to exploit its full economic potential. The Royal Geographic Society, founded in 1788 to explore and classify the uncharted regions of the world, sponsored British adventurers to fill in the blank spaces on European maps of Africa. Although many of these explorers were driven by a quest for knowledge and a romantic love of adventure, their expeditions were intended primarily to gather useful economic intelligence about the African interior. British commercial interests hoped to bypass the powerful coastal societies that had previously monopolized Africa's international trade.

It is therefore not surprising that Mungo Park and his contemporaries concentrated their efforts on mapping major African rivers that had the potential to become lucrative commercial arteries. Park, along with Hugh Clapperton, charted the upper and lower reaches of the Nile in the early decades of the nineteenth century. In East Africa, Richard Burton and John Speke reached Lake Tanganyika in the 1850s, and Samuel Baker confirmed that Lake Victoria/Nyanza was the source of the Nile in 1862. Lest there be any doubt that these expeditions had a commercial dimension, David Livingstone carefully noted regions that were well suited to sugar and cotton production during his exploration of the hinterlands of Central Africa in the 1850s. British-born explorers like Henry Stanley, who charted the Congo Basin for King Leopold of Belgium in the 1880s, saw no conflict of interest in working for foreign governments because they were confident that they were opening Africa for free British trade.

Surprisingly enough, the adventurers faced little active resistance from the African societies they encountered. Park, Clapperton, and Livingstone all died of disease on their travels; most of those who survived had the aid of cooperative Africans who provided them with food and guidance. Yet this hospitality did not mean that African states and societies were willing to allow the British merchants who followed in the explorers' wake to shift the terms of trade in their favor. In Central Africa, competition between the African Lakes Company and Afro-Arab traders in what is now northern Malawi led to the Slavers War of 1887. Although the Lakes company depicted the conflict as a crusade against slavery, in reality it was a struggle for control of the region's lucrative ivory trade.

Similarly, almost as soon as Park and Clapperton had established that the Niger River was navigable, a Liverpool commercial consortium made plans to bypass coastal African middlemen by using steamships to deal directly with commodity producers farther up the river. The Africa Inland Commercial Company's first expedition was decimated by disease in 1832, but twenty years later British river steamers became so prevalent in the Niger Delta that they were attacked by outraged African traders. Unwilling to tolerate such a flagrant violation of the principles of free trade, British palm oil traders convinced the British government to provide military support. A Royal Navy gunboat destroyed the offending villages, and by the 1870s armed steamers patrolled the river to discourage African attempts to reassert their commercial monopoly. Yet Britain's growing military supremacy did not allow it to dictate the terms of the palm oil trade entirely. When British merchants attempted to form a cartel to reduce palm oil prices, African producers retaliated with a trade embargo. Thus Africans could deal with European commercial interests on relatively equal terms as long they retained their sovereignty.

As has already been noted, British imperialists had no intention of annexing African territory before the late nineteenth century. During the era of free trade they calculated that even with the expansion of legitimate commerce, Africa's potential economic value did not justify the overall cost of its conquest and administration. The British government therefore relied largely on informal methods to further its African interests during the middle decades of the nineteenth century. In East Africa, it transformed Zanzibar into an unofficial British protectorate by using military intimidation to convince the sultan of Zanzibar to follow the advice of a British consul general.

With the exception of the Cape Colony in southern Africa, Britain's only formal African possessions at midcentury were in coastal West Africa. British traders had extensive commercial interests in the Gambia, Sierra Leone, Lagos, and the Gold Coast, but the British government's decision to transform these regions into formal crown colonies was based primarily on the requirements of the antislavery campaign. British abolitionists and Clapham philanthropists established a settlement at Freetown in Sierra Leone as a home for liberated slaves and the "black poor" of London in 1787. The latter group was composed largely of peoples of African descent who sided with loyalists during the American Revolution. Although the settlement initially faced considerable financial difficulties, it developed into the main center of operations for the West African antislaving campaign and became a crown colony in 1808.

Similarly, in the eighteenth century, British merchants had abandoned their long-standing trading enclaves on the Gambia River due to the French military threat and the intransigence of local African rulers. In 1816, the Royal Navy returned to the river to transform Banjul Island, renamed Bathurst after the British colonial secretary, into a base for the Anti-Slavery Squadron. The territory subsequently became a crown colony in 1821.

In what was to become Nigeria, similar commercial and strategic interests led Britain to annex the port town of Lagos in 1851. The town and its hinterlands became a crown colony ten years later when an alliance of palm oil traders and abolitionists convinced the British government that they needed official support to extend their influence into the interior.

On the Gold Coast, Britain became embroiled in a conflict with the powerful Asante Confederation over the administration of coastal trading forts in the 1820s. The confederation controlled the Akan goldfields, but by the nineteenth century Asante elites had become heavily involved in the slave trade. Angered by the attempts of British merchants and abolitionists to break their commercial monopoly by making alliances with their Fante rivals, the Asante fought several major wars with Britain during the middle decades of the nineteenth century. The confederation's acquisition of modern firearms through trade and rent on the coastal trading forts made it a potent foe. Therefore the British government did not try to impose its authority on the Asante until the era of informal empire drew to a close. The region became a crown colony only after a major British military expedition ended the confederation's hold on the coast in 1874.

It is clear that only humanitarian or strategic arguments could over-come Britain's reluctance to acquire African territory during the era of informal empire. British merchants had extensive trading interests up and down the West African coast but were able to convince the British government to intervene on their behalf only when they demonstrated that a region served a larger national interest. As was noted in chapter 1, Sir Charles Adderley and his anti-imperialist allies in Parliament argued that the four West African colonies were an unacceptable drain on the British Treasury because they only benefited a small group of exporters and traders. Adderley was unsuccessful, but he ensured that these four crown colonies received very little financial support from London. As a result, the administration of the West African territories was left largely in the hands of merchants, missionaries, and a handful of British officials. One of the main reasons for British expansion in Africa during the era of informal imperialism was that these "men on the spot" often exceeded their authority by embroiling the British government in local affairs in which it had no official interest.

The West African colonies survived in this climate of financial austerity and official indifference with the assistance of an influential class of westernized Africans who served as interpreters, commercial agents, commodity brokers, and civil servants. Many of these educated Africans came from well-established Afro-European communities that were the product of three centuries of interaction between European traders and the peoples of the West African coast. It was not unusual for visiting British sailors and merchants to marry local women, and members of local commercial classes often learned English and converted to Christianity to serve as middlemen in West Africa's international system of trade. One of the most successful of these families was the Brew family of the Gold Coast, who traced its ancestry to an eighteenth-century Irish merchant. Westernized Africans often sent their children to school in Britain as they became more prosperous, and they were well equipped to exploit the opportunities presented by the expansion of British imperial influence on the West African coast.

This Anglicized African community grew considerably in the nineteenth century with the establishment of Sierra Leone as a settlement for liberated slaves. The Africans rescued by the Royal Navy presented the abolitionist movement with a dilemma because few could return to their original homes. Some were enslaved as children, and others had been criminals or social outcasts. British evangelists hoped to use these displaced people to spread the gospel in Africa and purchased the land for the original settlement that became the city of Freetown. Over the course of the nineteenth century this community grew substantially with the return of former Yoruba slaves from Brazil and the Caribbean. British missionary societies established an extensive system of Western-style primary and secondary schools in Sierra Leone and the Gold Coast to facilitate their conversion and to prove that Africans in general were capable of assimilating Christian values. By midcentury, these schools had produced a class of Africans who embraced the values and material trappings of British culture.

Yet these "Afro-Victorians" were not simply black Englishmen. Sierra Leone was founded by African veterans of the British army, ex-squatters from Nova Scotia, and the "black poor" of London, in addition to liberated slaves. Most of these people were Christians, and in the 1790s they founded the first Western-style Christian church in Africa, predating the arrival of the first European missionaries by almost twenty years. Members of this Krio Church used high English for their religious services but spoke a hybrid of English and local African languages in their daily lives. They also followed African customs in circumcision and burial rites. These modifications made Christianity more accessible to the general African population, and the Afro-Victorians played a key role in spreading the new faith throughout the continent. The Church Missionary Society's mission to Nigeria was composed entirely of Africans under the leadership of Samuel Ajayi Crowther, who was the first African bishop ordained in the Anglican Church in 1864.

Afro-Victorians like Crowther did not participate in the colonial venture because they were the loyal pawns of British imperialists. They helped build Britain's African empire because they assumed, with good reason, that they would be its primary beneficiaries. Before Social Darwinism and pseudoscientific racism became popular in the late nineteenth century, Afro-Victorians made up a substantial segment of the colonial bureaucracy in Britain's West African colonies. They were cheaper and less vulnerable to disease than British civil servants, and many achieved senior positions in the colonial administration. Barrister Samuel Lewis was the first African to receive a knighthood, and James

Africanus Horton rose to the rank of lieutenant-colonel in the British army's medical service. Many of these Anglicized Africans genuinely believed that Africa would benefit from the "civilizing" influence of British rule, and editorials in African papers in the 1870s and 1880s joined with British merchants in calling on the government to annex the hinterlands of the West African colonies.

BRITAIN AND THE PARTITION OF AFRICA

As has already been noted, most Africans were caught off guard by the European partition of Africa in the 1880s. Britain and its allies had acquired a few strategically and economically important coastal enclaves over the course of the nineteenth century but had expressed no intention to divide up the entire continent. Even British imperialists themselves seemed unable to explain their sudden desire to acquire vast expanses of new territory with no apparent immediate value. As was pointed out in chapter 1, they were inspired primarily by changes taking place in Europe rather than Africa. Faced with the daunting prospect of a global depression and increased competition from foreign rivals, British merchants and manufacturers lobbied the government to take an active role in protecting and expanding their overseas markets.

It would therefore be tempting to explain Britain's active role in the partition of Africa as an effort to defend its informal empire by formal means. Unfortunately, recent historical research has shown that sub-Saharan Africa never accounted for more than 5 percent of Britain's total exports in the late nineteenth century. To be sure, desperate textile magnates, hit hardest by the depression of the 1870s, did hope that new African colonies would provide a captive and protected market for their products, but they lacked the political influence to dictate such a drastic revision in imperial policy. Although it could be argued that Britain annexed Egypt and South Africa to protect its extensive financial interests in these territories, this explanation does not work for the rest of Africa because British investors avoided risking their capital in the less developed regions of the continent.

It now seems clear that Britain's annexation of large sections of the African interior was inspired primarily by a combination of economic and strategic considerations linked to the increasing level of commercial and political competition in western Europe in the late nineteenth century. As the declining British manufacturing sector lost ground to continental and North American rivals, Britain became more dependent on international banking and other "invisible exports" to finance imports of food and raw materials. Although British bankers and investors concentrated on developing industrial economies in Europe, the Americas, and Australia, the pressure of increased international competition beginning in the 1870s forced them to consider the economic potential of sub-Saharan Africa and the other tropical regions of the world.

Yet few African societies were equipped structurally to provide suitable outlets for British trade and investment. With the exception of a handful of states on the West African coast, they lacked a uniform system of convertible currency, and most of their productive labor was devoted to pastoralism or subsistence agriculture. Many of these societies had developed complex systems of exchange to provide for their material wants, but they had little interest in wage labor, government loans, or railways. Thus the "new" imperialism in Africa can be interpreted as a speculative effort by Britain and the other imperial powers to restructure African societies to make them more receptive to European trade and investment. The African interior offered few prospects for immediate riches, but British imperialists considered their share of the continent to be a long-term investment. Merchants, long frustrated by the restrictive trade policies of coastal African states, warmly embraced their efforts. Charging that Africans could not manage commodity production on their own, they called for military intervention to force African societies to abolish their internal tariffs and honor commercial contracts and debts.

Nevertheless, mounting pressure from commercial and financial interests to transform African societies into suitable outlets for trade and investment was not enough to convince the British government to abandon its long-standing hostility to formal empire. It took the growing pressure of French and German imperialism to force Britain to defend its African interests. Egypt and South Africa attracted substantial levels of British investment, but they also sat astride strategically important routes to India. Some historians have argued that the British occupation of Egypt in 1882 touched off the "scramble for Africa" by signaling the French and the Germans that Britain intended to acquire an extensive African empire. With the discovery of extensive gold and diamond deposits in South Africa, no imperial power was willing risk missing out on similar riches in other corners of the continent. Moreover, the popularity of protective tariffs in continental Europe and North America raised the possibility that Britain's rivals would no longer abide by the principles of free trade in Africa. These fears compelled British imperialists to resort to formal empire to defend their interests, both real and speculative, in the African hinterland.

One of the main differences between Britain's conquest of India and its empire-building ventures in Africa was that it never sought to control the entire continent. British imperialists coveted regions that had strategic value, economic potential, or existing commercial interests. Although Britain and its rivals competed to acquire promising territories, they were not willing to allow their differences in Africa to lead to war in Europe. The major European powers therefore met in Berlin in 1884 to set the ground rules for the partition of Africa. The Berlin Conference established that an imperial power had to substantiate its territorial claims by demonstrating "effective administration" of the area in question, meaning that they had to convince African rulers to acknowledge their authority by signing a "treaty of protection."

Few Africans realized the full implications of these treaties. Those who lived in coastal regions had no idea that the terms of their long-standing commercial relations with Europe were about to change drastically. Africans in the interior viewed the British and their contemporaries as useful allies against local enemies. They failed to understand that their signatures (or the thumbprints that represented their signatures) on the treaties of protection would strip them of their sovereignty.

British imperialists often had to resort to military force to convince more hesitant African states and societies to surrender their economic and political autonomy. Whereas the British East India Company had needed vast sums of money and several hundred thousand soldiers to complete its century-long conquest of the Indian subcontinent, Britain used late-nineteenth-century advances in military technology to subdue its African colonies at a fraction of the cost in manpower and resources. Repeating rifles, lightweight field artillery, and the maxim gun (a precursor of the machine gun) allowed a handful of British troops to kill vast numbers of Africans at little risk to themselves. Furthermore, British imperialists reduced the cost of these operations by employing large numbers of inexpensive African soldiers and auxiliaries. As was the case in

India, they exploited social and political tensions to convince marginalized Africans to help colonize themselves.

Although many African states tried to keep pace with advances in military technology, the Brussels Treaty of 1890 banned the sale of modern rifles in sub-Saharan Africa. Thus in 1893 it took fifty members of the British South African Police just ninety minutes to slaughter approximately 3,000 Ndebele warriors in what is now Zimbabwe. The Ndebele had only short stabbing spears and shields to counter the six maxim guns used by the police. On the other hand, Africans could still overcome their technological inferiority by exploiting weak British leadership. In 1879, the Zulu killed some 1,600 British troops at the battle of Isandhlawana after a British general foolishly overextended his forces. These victories were short-lived, however, and no African state (save Ethiopia) was able to preserve its sovereignty by force of arms.

The relative ease with which British forces defeated Africans on the battlefield helped provide ideological legitimacy for the "new" imperialism. Imperial apologists cited their military and technological supremacy to support the Social Darwinists' depiction of Africans as culturally inferior. They viewed Britain's conquest of Africa as part of the process of "natural selection" by which superior nations dominated the "backward races" of the world. Even Evangelicals tended to accept this stereotype in arguing that formal British rule was needed to protect "childlike" Africans from unscrupulous European speculators and adventurers. This argument allowed British imperialists to portray themselves as altruistic humanitarians rather than self-interested conquerors.

Britain's new African subjects faced a difficult task in determining how to coexist with the new imperial order. In West Africa, Britain made little effort to expand its coastal enclaves in the Gambia and Sierra Leone but acquired the hinterlands of Lagos and the Gold Coast to protect its expanding commercial interests. In the former case, the British government relied on Sir George Goldie's Royal African Company to impose "effective administration" on what was to become Nigeria. Goldie used the West African Frontier Force, which was essentially his private army, to subdue the emirates of the Sokoto caliphate in 1897. He turned a profit by wresting control of the palm oil trade from local African merchants. The government tolerated Goldie's decidedly unfree trade practices because he checked French designs on the region and paid for the costs of its conquest and administration out of his own pocket.

In comparison, Britain could not rely on a chartered company to conquer the Gold Coast because the Asante Confederation was a much more formidable enemy. The Asante could muster an army of 20,000 men, and three battalions of the regular British army were required to break their hold on the coast in 1874. The resulting Treaty of Fomena forced the confederation to pay Britain an indemnity of 50,000 ounces of gold, but it retained its sovereignty for the time being. Yet the magnitude of the defeat sparked a crisis of confidence in Asante society. An influential segment of the ruling elite concluded that the only way to cope with the British threat was to depose the reigning Asantehene (head of state) and remodel the confederation along European lines.

Unfortunately, the new Asantehene's attempts to modernize the army and reform the penal code provoked serious social instability. The military and economic innovations that made British imperialism possible had significant social costs and could not be readily grafted onto existing African societies. Although reformers might eventually have succeeded in strengthening the confederation, Britain never gave them the chance to see their experiment through to the end. British imperialists exploited the confederation's weaknesses by making alliances with its vassal states, and the Asante had no choice but to submit to British protection themselves in 1896.

Most East African societies were even less equipped to cope with the "new" imperialism. The peoples of the hinterland had very little direct contact with the wider world before they were confronted with the partition. There were no European commercial enclaves in the region, and the coastal Swahili peoples were linked to the Islamic Middle East by religion and commerce. Yet the sultan of Zanzibar, an Omani Arab who claimed nominal sovereignty over the East African coast, actually facilitated the "scramble" for Africa. As an informal British client, he helped legitimize the partition by leasing what was to become the Kenyan coast to British commercial interests.

As was the case in West Africa, the British government had little interest in bearing the expense of acquiring formal colonies. Once Britain fixed the boundaries of what was to become British East Africa with its German rivals, it turned the administration of the territory over to Sir William MacKinnon's British East Africa Company. MacKinnon had vague but ambitious plans to develop the East African hinterland. His company, however, teetered on the brink of bankruptcy because the region lacked easily exploitable mineral resources, and local African economies were not suited to his needs. Few East Africans in the interior produced commodities for the world market, and MacKinnon could not emulate Goldie's success by capturing preexisting trade networks. He therefore hoped to secure a government subsidy for his empire-building activities. Normally, the British government would have refused to commit scarce public revenues to support such an unprofitable and ill-conceived private enterprise. Yet it needed MacKinnon to supply "effective administration" to establish Britain's claim to the region under the terms of the Berlin Conference.

More specifically, it hoped to use MacKinnon's company to extend British influence to Lake Victoria/Nyanza and the headwaters of the Nile. The kingdom of Buganda, a centralized African state on the northwestern shore of the lake, was a prize that attracted both Britain and its imperial rivals. In an effort to acquire Western technology and balance the growing influence of Muslim traders at his court, the kabaka (king) of Buganda opened his kingdom to Christian missionaries. His invitation attracted French and British missionary organizations who hoped to convert all of Bugandan society by gaining influence over the kabaka and his nobles. In the late 1880s, the resulting struggle between Protestant, Catholic, and Muslim factions among the Bugandan nobility plunged the kingdom into civil war. As was the case with the Asante, the kabaka's attempts to strengthen his realm by using Western ideas and technology produced serious social tensions that left his kingdom too weak to resist the expansion of British imperialism.

Frederick Lugard, a representative of the British East Africa Company, established British authority in Buganda by using a small African force backed by maxim guns to win the civil war for the Protestants. MacKinnon then pressured the British government to help develop his holdings by building a subsidized railway from the East African coast to Lake Victoria/Nyanza, and he threatened to withdraw from this strategically important region if he did not get assistance. Lord Rosebery, the British prime minister, believing that the security of British rule in Egypt depended on control of the Nile headwaters, declared Buganda a British protectorate in 1892. MacKinnon did not get his subsidy, but the British government rescued him from further losses by buying him out three years later.

The British East Africa Company begot the Uganda Protectorate and the East Africa Protectorate, which was subsequently renamed Kenya in 1920. The collapse of MacKinnon's chartered company left the administration of these territories in the hands of the British government. Lacking a monetarized economy and a well-established system of international trade that could be tapped through taxes and tariffs, both colonies threatened to become serious burdens to the British taxpayer. Colonial officials therefore decided to accelerate the economic transformation of the East African territories by using government funds to build MacKinnon's railway. Furthermore, they encouraged Europeans, mostly minor British aristocrats, to settle in the cool and fertile Kenyan highlands to ensure that the Uganda Railway would have paying customers.

This radical policy forced the British government to subdue the peoples of the Kenyan hinterland. Most of these societies had economies based on pastoralism or subsistence agriculture, and on the surface appeared to be much more poorly equipped than the Bugandans to come to terms with British imperialism. Yet their decentralized institutions of authority proved an advantage because there was no powerful head of state like the kabaka to sign away their sovereignty. Furthermore, they retained a higher degree of internal cohesion because they did not try to borrow the socially divisive products of Western culture and technology. In the end, however, these advantages were offset by Britain's military superiority and the unintentional introduction of infectious diseases such as smallpox that were rare in the East African hinterlands. Historians have estimated that the resulting famine and epidemics reduced the population of some ethnic groups by as much as 50 percent.

Nevertheless, some decentralized East African societies were better equipped than others to cope with the burdens and opportunities of British imperialism. For example, the Maasai and Nandi peoples adopted substantially different tactics to deal with the expansion of British authority despite the similarities in their pastoral and semipastoral economies. The Maasai, long-standing rivals of the Nandi, dominated the broad grasslands of the Rift Valley throughout most of the nineteenth century. Yet on the eve of the British conquest they were weakened substantially by a devastating civil war and a virulent cattle virus, known as rinderpest, which all but wiped out their primary means of subsistence. As a result, many Maasai warriors tried to rebuild their herds by serving British imperialists as "native auxiliaries" in return for a share of any livestock they captured. The Maasai became one of the few African societies to have their relations with Britain codified by treaty. British administrators subsequently broke these treaties by appropriating the central Rift Valley, but the Maasai retained title to the largest reserve of fertile land in colonial Kenya, despite the fact that they were one of the colony's smallest ethnic groups.

The Nandi, on the other hand, refused to compromise with the British imperialists. Even though their herds were also decimated by the rinderpest epidemic, the legacy of Afro-Arab slave traders left them suspicious of strangers. Inspired by a charismatic leader known as an orkoiyot, Nandi warriors used military force to interfere with the construction of telegraph lines and the Uganda Railway. After numerous "punitive expeditions" failed to convince the Nandi to cooperate, it took almost 4,000 colonial soldiers and 1,000 Maasai auxiliaries to break their resistance in 1905. In addition to killing six hundred Nandi warriors, the "Nandi field force" carried off approximately 10,000 head of cattle and almost 20,000 sheep and goats. The Nandi had little choice but to surrender or starve. The colonial government took so much of their land for European settlement that many Nandi had to turn to wage labor to survive.

The formal expansion of British imperialism in southern Africa followed a substantially different trajectory. Throughout most of the nineteenth century the British government struggled to find a means of assimilating the Afrikaner population it had inherited from the Dutch. The Afrikaners vehemently opposed Britain's attempts to Anglicize them by making English the language of administration in the Cape Colony. They considered British humanitarian criticism of their treatment of local Africans a threat to their way of life, and beginning in 1835 some 14,000 pioneers, known as *voortrekkers,* fled to the high grasslands of southeastern Africa to escape British rule. After defeating a powerful Zulu force at the Battle of Blood River in 1839, they founded the Transvaal and the Orange Free State as separate republics.

Although Britain recognized the independence of these governments under the Sand River Convention of 1852, British imperialists were unwilling to allow them enough autonomy to threaten the strategically important Cape Colony. The British government tried to keep the Afrikaners from having an outlet to the sea by encouraging British immigration in Natal and designating the region a crown colony. It also used humanitarian concerns over the poor treatment of local African societies as an excuse to intervene in the affairs of the Transvaal and the Orange Free State. These concerns, however, did not prevent them from fighting a series of wars with the Zulu and Xhosa peoples of Natal and the eastern Cape to protect British settlers and block the further expansion of Afrikaner influence. Other groups like the Sotho, when faced with the prospect of conquest by the Afrikaners, voluntarily sought British protection as the lesser of two evils.

The British government's willingness to extend its influence into South Africa's hinterland did not mean that it had abandoned its mid-century commitment to informal empire. Britain annexed coastal territory and established protectorates over local African societies as a relatively low-cost method of containing the Afrikaners. These measures were largely successful until prospectors discovered extensive deposits of diamonds and gold in the two republics, the Transvaal and the Orange Free State, in 1869 and 1886, respectively.

The British government became concerned that the Transvaal and the Orange Free State might eclipse the Cape Colony as the dominant political force in southern Africa as their lucrative mineral reserves attracted substantial amounts of foreign capital. Britain therefore sought to absorb the republics into a British-led South African federation by formally annexing the Transvaal in 1877. Yet the voortrekkers were no more willing to live under British rule in 1877 than they had been in 1836. Three years later the Afrikaners regained control of local affairs in the Transvaal by defeating a British force at Majuba Hill, but under the terms of the Pretoria Convention of 1881 Britain retained nominal control over their foreign relations.

This was the situation in southern Africa when Britain adopted a more expansionist imperial policy after the Conference of Berlin. Although there were considerable cultural differences between the Afrikaners and their African neighbors, British imperialists treated the Afrikaners as another African "tribe" in need of economic restructuring to favor British commercial interests. British investors supplied most of the capital to develop the southern African gold and diamond fields in the late nineteenth century but were frustrated by the restrictions that the republics placed on the mining industry. Led by Cecil Rhodes, the director of the British South Africa Company and prime minister of the Cape Colony, they pressed the British government to facilitate the economic development of the region by forcing the Afrikaner republics to be more responsive to their interests.

As the most influential of the mining magnates, Rhodes often pursued an independent imperialist agenda. He monopolized the Kimberley diamond mines in the Orange Free State and held a controlling interest in the Transvaal's Witwatersrand goldfields. In an effort to find more gold deposits and further isolate the Afrikaners, Rhodes secured an imperial charter for the central African territories that came to be known as Northern and Southern Rhodesia (modern Zambia and Zimbabwe). He used the British South Africa Company's private army of European adventurers and policemen to subdue the Shona and Ndebele and, unlike Goldie and MacKinnon, realized substantial profits by developing the region's gold, copper, and coal deposits. Believing that his personal fortune was tied to the expansion of the British Empire, he dreamed of a transcontinental railway linking Britain's African possessions from Cape Town to Cairo.

Therefore Rhodes was openly hostile to the Afrikaner governments of the Transvaal and Orange Free State. In 1895 he did his best to create an opportunity for Britain to annex the republics by allowing one of his underlings, Leander Starr Jameson, to instigate an uprising of foreign miners (known as Uitlanders) in the Transvaal. The Jameson Raid was a total failure because most miners were more interested in looking for gold than in fighting the Afrikaners, and it is tempting to blame Rhodes for the Anglo-Boer War of 1899–1902. J. A. Hobson, a contemporary journalist and critic of empire, charged that Rhodes and a shadowy cabal of capitalist investors instigated the war to protect their narrow economic interests. Yet there is little evidence to support this conclusion. The Afrikaners never threatened to shut down the mines, and many of Rhodes's fellow mining magnates did their best to avert the conflict because they correctly recognized that it would disrupt production.

Britain's decision to go to war with the Afrikaners was based primarily on concerns that its imperial rivals, particularly Germany, were gaining too much influence in the republics. The Germans had loaned the government of the Transvaal several million pounds to purchase weapons, there were over 5,000 German immigrants in the republics, and the kaiser had publicly congratulated the Afrikaners on defeating the

Jameson Raid. Britain feared that foreign support and the republics' vast mineral wealth would allow the Afrikaners to create a powerful South African union that would swallow the Cape Colony and Natal. Having failed to control the Afrikaners by less formal means, the British government resorted to armed force to unite southern Africa under a friendly government that it hoped would safeguard its considerable economic and strategic interests in the region.

The war itself provided Britain with a powerful lesson on the risks of formal empire. Although numerically superior, the British army was able to defeat the highly mobile and self-sufficient Afrikaner mounted forces only by cordoning off the countryside with a network of barbed wire and fortified blockhouses and by incarcerating their families in detention camps. Almost 34,000 Afrikaner soldiers were killed in the fighting, and approximately 20,000 women and children died of disease and neglect in the camps. The war cost Britain 22,000 casualties and over £200 million, roughly 14 percent of the nation's national income in 1902. It cost fifteen pence per head to subdue each of Britain's African subjects but over £1,000 for each Afrikaner defeated during the Anglo-Boer War.

Thus the partition of Africa was an extremely disruptive process that often entailed considerable bloodshed and social dislocation for Africans and Afrikaners alike. Although strategic concerns played an important role in the British government's shift to formal empire, for the most part, British imperialists sought to subordinate African societies to Britain's financial and commercial interests. Their superior military technology allowed them to deprive most Africans of their sovereignty with relative ease. Yet the expense of the South African war in human life and economic resources reminded British imperialists of the lessons learned from the Indian mutiny of 1857: the security and stability of their overseas empire depended on their ability to convince at least a small percentage of their colonial subjects of the value of British rule.

AFRICA UNDER BRITISH RULE

Once the partition of Africa drew to a close in the late nineteenth century, British imperialists were left with the problem of how to govern their new African empire. With the exception of the annexation of

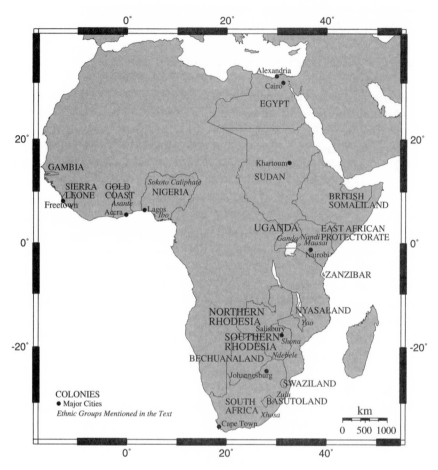

Map 4.1   British Africa, c. 1914

Egypt and South Africa, Britain's participation in the "scramble for Africa" was largely speculative. Although Cecil Rhodes and a handful of his contemporaries profited from the "new" imperialism, few African colonies offered even the slightest chance of an immediate return on the British government's imperial investment. As a result, the Treasury's emphatic prohibition on the use of metropolitan funds to subsidize colonial rule weakened the new African administrations severely.

With limited funds to pay British civil servants, policemen, and soldiers, colonial officials faced the difficult task of transforming the colonies into profitable enterprises without provoking an unmanageable backlash from their African subjects. In 1898, the three-year anticolonial uprising known as the Hut Tax War in Sierra Leone cost £45,000. Between 1895 and 1905, the East Africa Protectorate (Kenya) spent one-third of its total domestic revenues on "punitive operations" to force groups like the Nandi to pay their taxes. Most colonial governments did not have the resources to fight prolonged wars of pacification. Thus their financial limitations softened the impact of partition by creating substantial opportunities for Africans who were able to exploit these inherent contradictions in the imperial system.

British officials were influenced primarily by issues of cost and utility in designing an administrative system for Africa. Lacking even a rudimentary tax base, most colonies struggled to make do with extremely limited financial resources. With the exception of South Africa, few of Britain's new possessions attracted significant amounts of foreign investment, and only the West African territories had the basis of a viable export economy. Moreover, Britain's attempt to acquire an African empire on the cheap by relying on men like Goldie, MacKinnon, and Rhodes failed because their chartered companies could rarely survive without substantial government subsidies. Furthermore, the tendency of these private entrepreneurs to put profits ahead of the rights of their African subjects undermined the humanitarian ideals that legitimized the partition. By the turn of the century, mounting criticism over these private governments' excessive use of force compelled Britain to assume direct responsibility for its African colonies.

In most territories, British administrators, many of whom had served under the Raj, imported and adapted Indian models of indirect rule to Africa. They incorporated the rulers of strong centralized states like the Northern Nigeria emirates and the kingdom of Buganda directly into the colonial bureaucracy. Yet the Fulbe emirs and the Bugandan kabaka did not enjoy the autonomy of the Indian princes. These African leaders only retained control of local affairs, and British officials reserved the right to suppress any custom or institution that they deemed barbarous or uncivilized. Colonial administrators adapted the system of indirect rule to stateless African societies by transforming cooperative local dignitaries into "chiefs" and "headmen." Although they maintained the fiction that these "native authorities" had some form of "traditional" legitimacy, most were selected on the basis of their willingness to participate in the colonial system.

It is particularly interesting that Britain did not rely on Afro-Victorians to administer its West African colonies. Just as the leaders of the Raj blamed the Indian mutiny at least partially on the failure of Western-educated Indians to convince the general population of the benefits of British rule, colonial officials decided that Anglicized Africans were illegitimate in the eyes of "traditional" African society. The "trousered" African joined the Indian "babu" as a subject of scorn and ridicule. Although this shift can be attributed in part to the rise of pseudoscientific racism in Britain, it was equally due to the fact that Afro-Victorians punctured the myth of African backwardness that legitimized British imperialism.

Furthermore, humanitarian rhetoric about protecting "primitive" African societies did not prevent the British government from delegating its administrative responsibilities to British settlers in the highlands of east and central Africa. Colonial officials encouraged European immigration to the East Africa Protectorate, Nyasaland, and the Rhodesias to build a viable economic base and offset the costs of colonial administration. Although the African majority prevented them from granting these European communities responsible government, the settlers enjoyed unofficial representation on colonial legislative councils. The Uganda Protectorate, which never developed a significant settler population, was the only territory in the region in which British officials favored African interests by relying on indirect rule.

In South Africa, the expense and bloodshed of the Anglo-Boer War forced the British government to seek an accommodation with the Afrikaners at the expense of their African subjects. Under the terms of the Peace of Vereeniging in 1902, Britain granted the Afrikaners amnesty, civil autonomy, and £3 million in compensation for the loss of their property in return for an oath of allegiance to the king of Britain. Sir Alfred Milner, the high commissioner for South Africa, was willing to be magnanimous because he hoped increased British immigration and the expansion of English-style education would diminish the Afrikaners' political influence. His optimism was unfounded, however, because the Great Trek of 1836 had already shown that the Afrikaners were thoroughly resistant to Anglicization.

As tensions in Europe mounted in the decades before the First

World War, Britain could not afford to maintain a large and expensive military garrison in South Africa. The British government therefore came to terms with the Afrikaners. In 1910 Britain allowed the Afrikaner majority to dominate the new Union of South Africa, which finally combined the Cape Colony, Natal, Transvaal, and the Orange Free State into a single administrative entity. Ironically, Gen. Louis Botha, who had been commander in chief of Afrikaner forces during the war, became the Union's first prime minister. Political expedience also forced Britain to withdraw its protection of local African societies and allow the Afrikaners to settle the "native question" on their own terms. This retreat had severe repercussions in the Cape Colony, since the territory's property-based, nonracial franchise allowed almost 5 percent of the non-European population the right to vote. The new union government refused to recognize the citizenship of these African elites and gradually phased out their voting rights.

Britain's retreat from its humanitarian ideals in South Africa reflected one of the fundamental contradictions of the imperial system in Africa. British imperialists needed productive and reliable sources of revenue to govern their colonies effectively but did not have the means to impose their will on their Afrikaner and African subjects. With imperial subsidies out of the question, they desperately needed to develop the infrastructure of the colonies to attract foreign investment. Yet the political influence of metropolitan commercial and manufacturing interests barred them from promoting any African enterprise that might compete with British trade or industry. Colonial officials had to concentrate their efforts on developing export-driven economies that produced minerals and agricultural commodities for the world market. Although some administrators hoped that British settlers might fill this role, most colonial ventures were so undercapitalized that they had to rely on large amounts of inexpensive African labor to remain viable. This placed the colonial governments in the difficult position of trying to stimulate economic development without provoking widespread social disruption and unrest.

In West Africa, it did not take much effort for colonial officials to convince African farmers to grow cocoa, palm oil, and peanuts for export. It has already been noted that rising commodity prices in the early nineteenth century inspired many West Africans to embrace legitimate commerce. This trend continued into the first decades of the next century, and by 1915, Nigeria and the Gold Coast accounted for almost a quarter of the world's cocoa output. West African farmers were so efficient that the British government turned down Sir William Lever's request to establish palm oil plantations in Nigeria. The revenue generated by African commodity production created new markets for Britain's industrial exports and allowed British officials to rely on customs and export duties to cover the cost of colonial administration.

This system worked so well that the Gold Coast and Nigerian governments did not have to introduce direct taxation until the 1930s, but it was not easily adapted to Britain's other African colonies. With the exception of clove production on Zanzibar, few East African societies had grown commodities for export before the colonial era. In the hinterland, British officials tried to transform Bugandan notables into progressive landlords by granting them title to large tracts of land, but the Bugandans preferred to collect rents and proved no more responsive to the experiment than the Bengali Zamindars. The Ugandan government was free to encourage African agricultural production because the protectorate did not have a substantial European population. In the rest of British East and Central Africa, however, colonial officials tailored development policies to serve the needs of international mining interests and British settlers.

The British government supported a settler-based agricultural economy in the East Africa Protectorate (Kenya) for a variety of political and economic reasons. It cost the Treasury almost £9 million to build the Uganda railway, and British politicians hoped to recoup their expenses by encouraging European settlement. To accomplish this, they appropriated large sections of the territory's central highlands from their African owners. Imperial apologists justified the move by claiming that the land was largely uninhabited, but in reality the region's Kikuyu, Kalenjin (which included the Nandi), and Kamba owners had been reduced substantially by colonial wars, epidemics, and famine. Joseph Chamberlain, the British colonial secretary, even went so far as to offer the highlands to Theodor Herzl's Zionists, but influential settler leaders with connections in the House of Lords convinced colonial officials to favor members of the British gentry. By the turn of the century, would-be immigrants to the East Africa Protectorate had to demonstrate financial resources of at least £1,000. Few of these wealthy settlers had much practical agricultural experience, and the protectorate would probably have generated greater revenue through African commodity production.

In southern Africa, Rhodes's British South Africa Company governed the Rhodesias until the 1920s. Although the region's substantial mineral deposits helped the Company retain its charter after MacKinnon and Goldie were bought out by the British government, these deposits were not substantial enough to keep the territories solvent. Company officials therefore seized large tracts of African land to promote the development of a European agricultural sector. They made it easier for middle-class Britons to emigrate to Southern Rhodesia because they worried that the colony might be absorbed into South Africa as large numbers of Afrikaners migrated north after the Anglo-Boer War. Similarly, British planters acquired extensive coffee and cotton estates in the Shire highlands of the Nyasaland Protectorate (Malawi) by purchasing large tracts of land, which had been depopulated substantially by a half century of slave raiding, from local Yao chiefs. The South African and Northern Rhodesian economies, on the other hand, remained tied primarily to the mining industry.

British administrators hoped European agricultural and mining interests would provide a solid foundation for colonial economic development. Yet few of these enterprises lived up to expectations because they were undercapitalized and lacked the basic infrastructure to produce reasonably priced exports for the world market. Their only hope of compensating for prohibitively high production and transportation costs was to rely on cheap African labor. Even South African mining companies, which controlled some of the world's richest gold and diamond reserves, depended on inexpensive African miners to turn a profit. Furthermore, the colonial governments themselves had to rely on low-cost African labor to make up for their lack of funding for public works. They needed Africans to build the roads, railways, and harbors that constituted the infrastructure of an export-based economy.

Yet most Africans in the early colonial era had little interest in paid employment. With the exception of the small class of West African commodity producers, many came from relatively self-sufficient pastoral and subsistence-oriented agricultural societies and were willing to sell their labor only to acquire specific material luxuries. Therefore colonial officials often resorted to drastic measures to produce laborers for settler farms, mines, and public works. In the first decades after partition they simply forced Africans to work; West African governments even tolerated the continued existence of slavery out of fears that universal emancipation would disrupt commodity production. Colonial officials postponed the moral crusade of the abolitionists, which was one of the main legitimizing ideologies of the imperial enterprise, to achieve specific economic goals. Ultimately, they let the institution die a gradual death by outlawing slave trading and encouraging individual slaves to purchase their freedom.

These were only short-term solutions, however, and colonial administrators developed more acceptable methods of encouraging Africans to work as humanitarian criticism of forced labor mounted in the first decades of the twentieth century. They restructured local African economies through a program of land alienation, punitive fines, and coercive taxation. Most British colonies imposed "head" taxes on able-bodied adults and "hut" taxes on African residences to increase government revenues and force Africans to earn money. As a whole, these taxes usually amounted to the equivalent of one to two months of paid labor.

In eastern and southern Africa, where settler and mine owner demand for African labor was particularly intense, colonial officials adopted even more invasive tactics. Military "pacification" campaigns punished tax resisters by seizing their livestock and burning their crops. Moreover, the East Africa Protectorate and the Union of South Africa established a system of "native reserves" that were not unlike Indian reservations in the United States. The South African Natives Land Act of 1913 confined the African majority, which constituted over 70 percent of the population, to just 13 percent of the union's arable land. Africans constituted over 80 percent of the population of the East Africa Protectorate, but only 20 percent of the colony's productive land was devoted to native reserves. Yet the small European settler community did not need these vast stretches of territory. The primary function of the native reserve system was to force Africans to become wage laborers by restricting their ability to practice subsistence agriculture.

By restructuring regional African economies through taxation and land appropriation, the colonial governments set in place a system that compelled Africans to travel great distances to earn enough money to pay their taxes and provide for their basic needs. Their main destinations were settler farms in the East Africa Protectorate and Southern Rhodesia, and gold and diamond mines throughout southern Africa. Strict racial segregation, known as the color bar, prevented African labor migrants from settling with their families in the European areas in which they were employed. Colonial officials argued that this policy prevented the disintegration of backward "tribal" societies, but in reality it kept wages low by forcing Africans to maintain ties to their rural homes. In other words, the wives and families of African labor migrants had to grow enough food to absolve European farmers and mine owners from having to pay their workers a living wage.

THE CONSEQUENCES OF BRITAIN'S AFRICAN EMPIRE

It is now easy to comprehend why the extension of formal British imperialism was so traumatic for so many Africans. Caught off guard by the unexpected shift in their relations with Europe or by the sudden discovery of militaristic Europeans (in the case of many hinterland societies), Africans struggled to cope with the alien nature of British imperial rule. Many shared the profound sense of dislocation and loss experienced by the Ibo village of Umuofia in Chinua Achebe's classic *Things Fall Apart*. In the novel, Okonkwo, a man of considerable means and influence, is stripped of his status and dignity by the new imperial order and finally commits suicide after murdering an African servant of the new colonial regime.

Yet the African response to formal British imperialism was far from uniform. Many African societies did rebel violently when confronted with the colonial state's demand for land, taxes, and forced labor. In 1896, the Ndebele and Shona killed over six hundred Europeans in a bloody guerrilla war, known as the Chimurenga, against the British South Africa Company. The Asante followed a similar course in 1900 after learning the full implications of being a British protectorate. Although these anticolonial uprisings occasionally managed to force administrators to temper specific policies, they also exposed rebellious African societies to the full retaliatory force of armed British imperialism. Over 9,000 Shona and Ndebele men, women, and children died during the Chimurenga, which was a tragic price to pay for temporarily slowing the rate of European settlement in the colony.

The Afro-Victorians, on the other hand, had more success in using British humanitarian ideology to oppose the most invidious aspects of colonial rule. The Aborigines Rights Protection Society and the Peoples Union of Lagos lobbied the metropolitan British government successfully to block attempts by colonial administrators to appropriate all uncultivated land in the Gold Coast and Nigeria. In southern Africa, however, humanitarian appeals had far less impact on the Afrikaner-dominated government of the Union of South Africa, and the South African National Congress made little headway in blocking the Natives Land Act of 1913.

Faced with increased discrimination under the color bar, frustrated African intellectuals turned to religion and racial solidarity to oppose colonial rule. In West Africa, John Africanus Horton and Edward Blyden conceived Pan-Africanism as a response to the colonial depiction of Africans as racially inferior. Educated African Christians also founded their own independent churches as an alternative to the European missions.

Although these forms of African physical and intellectual resistance to British imperialism were widespread and often intense, they were too dispersed and uncoordinated to be effective. In spite of the best efforts of the Pan-Africanists, distinctions in language, religion, and ethnicity prevented Africans from mounting a serious challenge to foreign rule. Furthermore, the weakness of most territorial governments actually strengthened the colonial system. Without the financial resources and manpower to rule Africa directly, British officials could not govern without the cooperation of at least a segment of African society. African chiefs and headmen filled the lower levels of the colonial bureaucracy, and the Christian missions, which ran more than 80 percent of the schools in Anglophone Africa, provided a new class of educated Africans with the means to advance in colonial society. Even the African poor found opportunities in the restructured colonial economy. Taxation and forced labor were undeniably oppressive, but British rule also gave farmers greater access to world markets and ultimately raised the price of African labor. It is illustrative that large numbers of Africans willingly migrated to Britain's West African colonies from neighboring French territories and, in Central Africa, from Portuguese Mozambique to British Nyasaland.

Moreover, the system of indirect rule created specific opportunities for Africans who successfully depicted themselves as "traditional" rulers. Colonial officials believed all Africans belonged to a "tribe," which can be defined loosely as a lower order of political and social organization that was less than a nation. Most precolonial ethnic identifications were determined by specific economic and environmental circumstances, with Africans acquiring new "tribal" identities through intermarriage, drought, migration, and slavery. Indirect rule ended this flexibility by making the "tribe" the main unit of colonial administration. As was the case in India, rigid ethnic categories helped the British understand the alien beliefs and values of their non-Western subjects. Therefore "traditional" authority was one of the most effective keys to unlocking the opportunities of the colonial system, and many Africans manipulated and recast their "tribal" identities to exploit the ignorance of colonial administrators. Chiefs and headmen interpreted African "tradition" for their British sponsors, and many acquired considerable social status by codifying marriage and inheritance customs to give themselves authority over women and younger men.

By creating incentives for a limited number of Africans to participate in the colonial system, British officials simultaneously reduced the cost of imperial rule and diluted the effectiveness of African resistance. To be sure, those Africans who cooperated with British imperialism often found themselves in the difficult position of having to enforce unpopular colonial policies. Although British administrators and an earlier generation of historians celebrated these African chiefs and bureaucrats as sensible mordernizers who recognized the value of European civilization, many nationalist historians in the postcolonial era branded them as traitors. In hindsight, however, neither description is particularly accurate. British imperialism destroyed the precolonial political and social order in Africa. Faced with the unexpected loss of their sovereignty, Africans struggled to cope with the realities of alien rule. What nationalist historians have described as "collaboration" was instead an attempt to retain as much autonomy as possible by exploiting the opportunities of imperial rule.

SUGGESTIONS FOR FURTHER READING

Achebe, Chinua. *Things Fall Apart*. New York: Fawcett Crest, 1984.
Boahen, A. A. *African Perspectives on Colonialism*. Baltimore: Johns Hopkins University Press, 1987.

Bridges, Roy C. "The Historical Role of British Explorers in East Africa." *Terrae Incognitae* 14 (1982): 1–21.

Dewey, Clive, and A. G. Hopkins. *The Imperial Impact: Studies in the Economic History of Africa and India*. London: Athlone, 1978.

Hopkins, A. G. *The Economic History of West Africa*. New York: Columbia University Press, 1973.

Kennedy, Dane. *Islands of White: Settler Society and Culture in Kenya and Southern Rhodesia, 1890–1939*. Durham, N.C.: Duke University Press, 1987.

Thompson, Leonard. *A History of South Africa*. New Haven: Yale University Press, 1995.

Vail, Leroy, ed. *The Creation of Tribalism in Southern Africa*. Berkeley: University of California Press, 1989.

White, Landeg. *Magomero: Portrait of an African Village*. Cambridge: Cambridge University Press, 1987.

5

BRITISH IMPERIAL INFLUENCE IN CHINA AND THE OTTOMAN EMPIRE

In the previous two chapters it was shown how Britain formalized and expanded its formal imperial control over India and Africa in response to regional tensions, domestic economic changes, and increased competition from its European rivals in the late nineteenth century. Although these same factors led British imperialists to seek greater influence in the Chinese and Ottoman Empires, it is important to explore why the Chinese and Ottomans did not suffer the fate of the Indians and Africans in becoming formal British subjects. With the exception of Egypt and South Africa, these two great non-European empires were far more economically valuable to Britain than any of its new African colonies. The substantial Chinese and Ottoman standing armies were so antiquated by the mid-nineteenth century that they were easily vanquished by smaller European forces equipped with modern weapons. On the surface, both societies appear to have been ripe for partition and annexation under the "new" imperialism.

Although the Chinese and Ottoman Empires eventually collapsed under the weight of their own internal tensions in the early twentieth century, they did not surrender their sovereignty to Britain. Ironically, both empires depended on British military and political support to avoid being partitioned by Britain's imperial rivals. Historians have offered a number of explanations for Britain's reluctance to add China or the Ottomans to its formal empire. Some have suggested that British imperialists did not want to acquire responsibility for governing more non-European subjects after the trauma of the Indian Mutiny of 1857, but this makes little sense in light of Britain's active role in the partition of Africa. It could also be argued that the Chinese and Ottoman economies did not require substantial restructuring to become suitable outlets for British commerce and finance, but British merchants in China often echoed their West African colleagues in demanding government intervention to force the Chinese to open their markets.

Most of these theories are unsatisfactory because they focus on British motives rather than on Chinese and Ottoman responses to imperialism. Indians and Africans were divided by ethnicity, caste, and religion, but the social cohesion of the Chinese and Ottomans offered greater protection from the "new" imperialists. Even though the Ottoman and Chinese Empires were in advanced stages of decay during the imperial century, they retained enough economic and social vitality to give the majority of their citizens little reason to cooperate with British imperialism. Although Britain could have defeated both empires on the battlefield (and did so on many occasions in China, with the assistance of the Indian army), Chinese and Ottoman cultural solidarity prevented British imperialists from using indirect rule effectively. Without the aid of a sufficient number of locally recruited soldiers, policemen, clerks, and headmen, Britain did not have the resources or manpower to govern these non-Western empires directly. Instead, British imperialists relied on informal influence to protect their interests in China and the Ottoman Empire at a time when they were partitioning Africa with their imperial rivals. Thus the Chinese and Ottoman cases illustrate how non-Western peoples could retain a degree of sovereignty by resisting the pressures of formal European imperialism.

THE GREAT NON-WESTERN EMPIRES

Although there were substantial differences between the Chinese and Ottoman Empires, both societies shared a number of characteristics that allowed them to resist the formal expansion of British imperialism. Boasting populations of 35 million Ottomans and over 400 million Chinese in the mid-nineteenth century, they had complex economies based on subsistence and commercial agriculture, extensive internal markets, and sophisticated handicraft industries. These economies became lucrative outlets for British trade and investment, but they were highly resistant, particularly in China, to forced restructuring by external interests. Furthermore, both empires had strong unifying ideologies that made it difficult for British imperialists to find enough local allies to make colonial rule practical.

For the most part, the Chinese considered themselves culturally superior to all foreign visitors. With a sense of continuity generated by a culture that had existed for thousands of years, they believed that their numbers, military power, economic vitality, technological achievements, and Confucian ideals made Chinese culture the embodiment of civilization. Every other society, regardless of its accomplishments, was barbarous in comparison. The few foreign invaders who managed to conquer China during the course of its long history had abandoned their own language and cultural institutions to govern the vast Chinese population, as illustrated by the Manchu nomads who overthrew the Ming dynasty in the mid-seventeenth century. Their new Ch'ing dynasty co-opted Confucianism as a ruling ideology and governed through the existing Chinese bureaucracy.

Although the Ch'ing emperors never lost the taint of their foreign origins in the eyes of the general population, it took only a few generations for them to become culturally Chinese. Moreover, Chinese elites rarely questioned Ch'ing legitimacy while China was the dominant East Asian economic and political power in the seventeenth and eighteenth centuries.

China's considerable cultural self-confidence was a powerful counterweight to British imperialism. Assuming that the desirability of high-quality Chinese products would force foreign merchants to trade on their terms, the Chinese adopted a xenophobic commercial policy that quarantined European traders in the southern port of Canton. As "barbarians," British merchants had no rights or status in China and were forced to contract with local Cantonese agents, known as Hongs, to acquire the goods they sought. Confined to specific trading factories called "barbarian houses" by the Chinese, British merchants had little contact with the general population. They were permitted to have only eight Chinese male servants, were barred from learning Chinese, and could communicate with governmental officials only through the head Chinese commercial agent in Canton. These restrictions served two purposes. First, they allowed the Chinese government and its agents to levy substantial fees and tariffs on foreign trade, and second, they limited the contaminating influence of the Europeans.

The Ottomans could not match the sheer size of the Chinese Empire but derived a similar degree of cultural self-confidence from their Islamic faith. In addition to creating a sense of moral and spiritual superiority over Christian Europe, Islam provided the Turkish sultans with political legitimacy. Taking their name from Osman, a thirteenth-century clan leader from what is now Turkey, the Ottomans captured Constantinople in 1453 and built a realm stretching from North Africa to the Black Sea. Their siege of Vienna in 1683 demonstrated that Ottoman armies were a match for any contemporary European power. This military dominance was built on a three-legged economic base of tribute, subsistence and commercial agriculture, and control of eastern Mediterranean trade routes.

Unlike the Chinese, the Ottomans built a multiethnic empire that included a substantial number of Jews and Christians. Although Islam was the political cornerstone of the empire, Islamic law did not require the sultans to convert these "peoples of the book" *(dhimmis)* to Islam. The main exception was the Corps of Janissaries, which formed the core of the Ottoman military. It was composed of military slaves captured as children in the Christian Balkans and raised as Muslims. To govern the majority of their non-Muslim subjects, the Ottomans developed a pragmatic system that granted limited administrative autonomy to the Greek Orthodox, Armenian Christian, and Jewish minorities. Each community, known as a millet, paid higher taxes in return for local control over their educational institutions, legal system, and religious affairs.

Unlike Mughal India, which was also an Islamic state, the millets gave the Ottoman Empire a degree of internal cohesion. Confident in their moral and military superiority, the Ottomans allowed Western merchants to establish tax-exempt commercial enclaves throughout the empire. With the aim of stimulating trade, they exempted these foreigners from Ottoman law by placing them under the extraterritorial legal protection of their own ambassadors and consuls. These concessions, which came to be known as capitulations, granted Westerners considerably more autonomy than did China's Canton system, but the Ottomans did not worry about their potentially divisive impact as long as they enjoyed economic and technological parity with Europe.

Both systems for controlling foreigners began to crumble on the eve of the imperial century. Internal economic and political tensions made it much harder for the Ottoman and Chinese Empires to keep pace with the burgeoning commercial and industrial power of Europe. Population pressure in China led to the division of peasant farms into small, nonviable parcels, and many peasants became tenant farmers. By the beginning of the nineteenth century, a handful of rich families controlled more than half of the arable land in China. The Ch'ing emperors did not interfere because they could not afford to alienate the landlord class, which produced the scholarly bureaucrats who ran the empire. As a result, the Ch'ing were so preoccupied with these internal problems that they considered the expansion of British influence a relatively minor problem. Alarmed by growing unrest in the countryside, the Ch'ing concentrated on maintaining the support of the landlord-scholar ruling class. In doing so, they neglected China's extensive irrigation and transportation infrastructure and failed to modernize its armed forces.

By comparison, Ottoman internal problems were even more pronounced. By the late eighteenth century, the Janissaries had become a well-entrenched interest group that blocked all attempts to modernize the Ottoman armed forces. This was a serious development because much of the empire's prosperity depended on the tribute generated by new conquests. The second and third legs of their economic base also grew weaker as Europe opened new maritime trade routes to Asia that bypassed the eastern Mediterranean.

This social and economic stagnation had dangerous political repercussions. Provincial Ottoman bureaucrats often became autonomous rulers as the sultans lost control of their more remote possessions. In the early nineteenth century, Muhammad Ali, an Albanian-born Ottoman general, transformed Egypt into a powerful state that remained a province of the empire in name only. At the same time, many of the millets sought to reassert their independence. The Ottomans were uncomfortably close to the centers of European imperialism and could not prevent the major Western powers from supporting the nationalist aspirations of their non-Muslim subjects.

The growing weakness of the Chinese and Ottoman Empires in the early nineteenth century created new opportunities for Britain. British commercial interests hoped to tap the vast internal markets of non-Western empires once the administrative and social barriers that had previously restricted European merchants to isolated enclaves began to crumble. Although their industrial supremacy gave them the means to win on the battlefield, few British imperialists seriously considered annexing the Ottomans or Chinese. They sought to use diplomatic influence and the judicious application of military force, or at least the threat of it, to wring specific economic and political concessions from the two non-Western empires.

BRITISH IMPERIALISM IN CHINA

Although China never became part of the British Empire, it played an integral role in Britain's informal network of imperial finance. In the eighteenth century, Britain had difficulty finding the resources to meet its growing taste for Chinese tea. Lacking sufficiently enticing products, the British East India Company purchased Chinese goods with silver

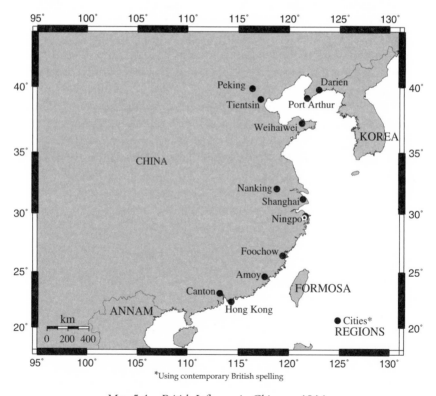

Map 5.1   British Influence in China, c. 1914

bullion. The Company alleviated this imbalance, which amounted to several million pounds per year at the turn of the century, by exporting Indian commodities to China. Just as the Chinese government maintained total control over all foreign trade in Canton, the Company monopolized Sino-Indian commerce by virtue of its royal charter. Any private British merchant wishing to carry Indian goods to China in what was known as the "country trade" had to purchase a special license. More importantly, company officials used their commercial contacts to export Indian revenues to Britain in the form of Chinese tea and textiles.

India's primary exports to China included raw cotton, ivory, sandalwood, and, most importantly, opium. Blessed with a sophisticated indigenous handicraft industry that produced valuable commodities like silk and porcelains and an enormous internal economy, the Chinese had little interest in trading for the simple manufactures of preindustrial Europe. It took a highly addictive drug like opium to redress Britain's Chinese trade deficit. The British East India Company loaned Indian peasants money to grow poppies and circumvented China's ban on opium imports by using the private country traders to sell the processed narcotic to Chinese middlemen. This illicit commerce earned the Company 30 million rupees in 1838; by the 1850s, opium sales accounted for almost 12 percent of the BEIC's total revenues.

Opium dealing by the British East India Company attracted little criticism in Britain outside of evangelical circles, but the Company's collaboration with the Chinese government in channeling all foreign commerce through Canton drew the ire of free traders. Hoping to gain access to hundreds of millions of potential customers, free traders became less interested in China as a source of raw materials and more interested in it as an outlet for British manufacturers. Missionaries, confined to Canton and the coastal enclave of Portuguese Macao, supported their efforts, hoping that increased commerce would allow them greater freedom to seek converts among the general Chinese population.

Free traders and their allies stripped the British East India Company of its commercial monopoly in 1833 but had far less success in convincing the Chinese to dismantle the Canton system. With the Company finally out of the picture, independent British traders founded powerful commercial firms that had little patience for bureaucratic restrictions on their activities. They lobbied London to intervene on their behalf, and Lord William Napier, Britain's chief superintendent of trade in China, tried to force the governor-general of Canton to relax the restrictions on foreign merchants. In response, the Chinese quarantined Britain's commercial enclaves. Faced with the prospect of bankruptcy, British traders had no choice but to convince their government to recall Napier.

Free traders might have had more success prying open Chinese markets if their primary import had not been opium. As millions of Chinese became addicts, China's international balance of trade shifted from a $26 million surplus in the 1810s to a $38 million deficit just twenty years later. The Chinese government therefore had little choice but to crack down on the illegal opium trade. In 1839, it prosecuted Chinese dealers, executed addicts, and blockaded the Canton trading enclaves to force foreign merchants to surrender their stocks of the narcotic. Lin Tse-hsu, the imperial commissioner in Canton, wrote an impassioned letter to Queen Victoria in 1840 defending his government's actions: "Suppose there were people from another country who carried opium for sale to England and seduced your people into buying and smoking it; certainly your honorable ruler would deeply hate it and be bitterly aroused." In taking this defiant stance, the Chinese made the same miscalculation that many African rulers would make forty years later. Unaware that industrial developments in Europe had tipped the military balance of power against them, they assumed Britain's insatiable appetite for Chinese products would force the British government to back down.

British merchants and politicians, on the other hand, depicted the dispute as a defense of free trade rather than a moral question of a sovereign nation's right to control opium smuggling. Encouraged by petitions from over three hundred metropolitan commercial firms, Lord Palmerston, the British foreign secretary, ordered the Royal Navy to blockade the coast to force the Chinese government to pay reparations for the destroyed opium. In 1842, backed by sepoys of the Indian army, armored British steamers forced their way up the Yangtze River to blockade China's major inland waterway, known as the Grand Canal. Facing a severe disruption of its internal commerce, the Chinese government negotiated a settlement with Britain.

Under the terms of the 1842 Treaty of Nanking and the 1843 Treaty of the Bogue, the Chinese paid an indemnity of $21 million ($6 million specifically for opium losses), abolished the Canton system, opened four new trading ports (Amoy, Foochow, Ningpo, and Shanghai), and ceded Hong Kong directly to Britain. The treaties also set import tariffs at a uniform 5 percent and, most importantly, granted all British citizens extraterritorial legal protection. This last measure became a cornerstone of informal British influence in China. It allowed merchants and missionaries to operate freely without the threat of persecution by the Chinese government.

The Chinese did not surrender such a large measure of their sovereignty willingly, and renewed tensions over these extraterritorial concessions were inevitable. In 1856, the Royal Navy shelled and occupied Canton in response to the Chinese government's seizure of a vessel flying a British flag. Although Britain had to postpone further military action to deal with the Indian Mutiny, it mounted a joint expedition with the French in 1858 to force the Chinese to stop interfering with European merchants. The Anglo-French force seized the Teku forts at the mouth of the Hai River, thereby laying Peking open to a "barbarian" invasion. The resulting Treaty of Tientsin forced the Chinese to open ten more ports to foreign trade, pay substantial indemnities, and allow all Westerners (including missionaries) to travel freely in China.

The collapse of the Canton system opened new opportunities for British commercial interests. Under British rule Hong Kong became an important entrepôt for goods destined for the Chinese hinterland. In just sixty years it grew from a population of just 15,000 (in 1841) to almost 300,000 residents. In Canton and the fourteen other treaty ports, powerful British trading houses like Dent and Company and Jardine, Matheson and Company diversified their interests, moving into tea processing, silk reeling, shipping, brewing, insurance, and money lending.

Even though China retained nominal sovereignty over these Western commercial bridgeheads, European merchants and consuls quickly took responsibility for their day-to-day administration. The foreign community in Shanghai grew into an "international settlement" with the local British consul assuming most of the responsibilities of city government. When a rebel Chinese group known as the Small Sword Society drove Ch'ing customs officials from the city in 1854, the British consul and the local U.S. commissioner collected the Chinese government's customs duties from Western traders operating in the region. Recognizing the need for a central authority to organize trade, British officials expanded the scope of this maritime customs service to include the entire coast. The Chinese government saw no contradiction in relying on foreigners to control foreigners and found the service's employees less prone to smuggling and embezzlement than its own customs officials. By end of the nineteenth century, the customs service's British director and staff of 3,000 (composed of both Chinese and Westerners) provided the Chinese government with approximately 20 percent of its total revenues.

Yet the treaty ports would not have been economically viable without Chinese assistance. All of the great trading houses depended on a staff of Chinese compradors to serve as brokers, translators, and clerks. The term "comprador" came from the Portuguese word *compra* "to buy." Chinese middlemen had played an important intermediary role in the Canton system for centuries but had little freedom to branch out on their own. The expansion of foreign authority in the treaty ports gave them much greater autonomy. The most successful compradors transformed themselves from employees of British commercial forms into independent brokers who collected Chinese commodities for export and helped local buyers secure credit to purchase foreign goods. Many learned English and adopted Western styles of dress to build cultural ties with their foreign partners. In doing so, they also acquired British nationality to secure extraterritorial protection from the Chinese government, which still sought to curtail the spread of Western influence.

Historians have disagreed considerably over the long-term influence of the Chinese compradors and the treaty ports. One school of thought holds that the Western commercial enclaves were "beachheads of imperialism" that broke down trade barriers and eroded China's sovereignty by allowing foreign interests access to its internal markets. Yet the overall impact of the treaty ports was quite limited. Powerful British trading houses made substantial profits in China, but their influence rarely extended beyond the coast. Moreover, although the Treaties of Nanking and Tientsin allowed Christian missionaries to operate freely in China, the evangelists won few converts among the general population. The treaty ports' true beneficiaries were the Chinese compradors, who profitably exploited their position as economic and cultural intermediaries.

Many British merchants pressured their leaders to use military force to open China's enormous internal markets. Yet the main commercial firms in the treaty ports had very little political influence in Britain because China never became an important outlet for British products. Its vast internal economy was largely self-contained throughout the imperial century, and opium remained Britain's must profitable Chinese import until the 1890s. In the absence of a viable transportation and distribution system, regional Chinese handicraft industries competed successfully with British manufacturers because they had better access to local markets. In 1903, almost 50 percent of China's imports came from the greater British Empire (including India), but this amounted to an extremely small fraction of Britain's total international trade. Therefore, few British politicians were willing to incur the considerable expense of adding large sections of Chinese territory to their formal empire.

Moreover, although Royal Navy gunboats could dominate the lower reaches of China's major rivers, Britain did not have the manpower (even with the Indian army), resources, or inclination to fight a major war on the Chinese mainland. On the contrary, most British imperialists recognized the value of preserving the viability of the Ch'ing dynasty. With no desire to assume responsibility for governing millions of Chinese, their goal was to coerce the Ch'ing emperors into opening their markets without destabilizing the Chinese government any more than necessary. Instead of exploiting Chinese weakness, Britain worked actively to defend the Ch'ing from their internal enemies and rival European imperial powers once it had dismantled the Canton system.

Beginning in 1850, the Chinese government began to lose control over large sections of southeastern China as a result of the Taiping Rebellion. Rebel leader Hung Hsiu-ch'uan, a failed Confucian scholar and a former student of an American Baptist mission, attracted hundreds of thousands of followers to a movement that embodied the cultural ramifications of foreign influence by combining a peasant revolt, an anti-Ch'ing backlash, and a pseudo-Christian crusade. Over the course of the fourteen-year uprising the Taipings caused the death of approximately 20 million people in sixteen provinces, destroyed hundreds of cities, and held Nanking for almost eleven years.

Clearly, the rebels provided Britain with an ideal opportunity to dismember the Chinese Empire. Yet the British government had little interest in doing so. British traders disliked the Taiping ban on opium, and missionaries distrusted his mixing of Christian and Confucian ideology. Recognizing that its commercial interests in China required internal stability, Britain backed the efforts of a Chinese militia under the command of Charles Gordon, a British adventurer who would later gain fame and martyrdom in the Sudan, to protect Shanghai from the Taipings.

Britain's commitment to informal empire allowed the Chinese to deal with the Taiping rebels without having to worry about foreign threats to their sovereignty. Yet, as noted in previous chapters, British imperialists could not rely on informal measures to protect their interests when faced with serious competition from rival powers. As latecomers to the imperial contest, France, Russia, Germany, and Japan did not share Britain's aversion to formal empire. By the 1880s, all four nations began to exploit China's military weakness by annexing its peripheral territories. France seized the Vietnamese province of Annam in 1884 while the Russians expanded their influence in Sinkiang (the western region). The Japanese, former vassals of the Ming dynasty, followed a particularly aggressive policy toward China in the late nineteenth century. After invading the island of Formosa (modern Taiwan) in 1874, they went to war with China over Korea in 1894. The Chinese were troubled by the loss of these peripheral regions, but the real threat came in the peace treaties that followed each military defeat. The victorious imperial powers invariably demanded exorbitant indemnities and exclusive economic concessions that undermined China's sovereignty substantially.

British imperialists had little choice but to join in this "scramble for concessions." Foreign traders of every nationality profited when Britain forcibly dismantled the Canton system after the Opium Wars, but the new concessions won by its imperial rivals threatened to exclude British merchants and investors. In 1897, Germany used the murder of two German missionaries to extort a ninety-nine-year lease on the northern Chinese port of Kiaochow while the Russians seized Port Arthur and Dairen. Both powers declared the immediate hinterland of these ports as their exclusive "sphere of influence." The French and Japanese quickly followed suit by acquiring similar concessions in Kwangchow Bay and Fukien province respectively.

These spheres of influence were a direct threat to Britain's informal empire in China. As has already been noted, the great British trading houses diversified their interests by developing shipping, insurance, and banking interests along the Chinese coast. Moreover, London financiers hoped to loan the Chinese government money to pay its indemnities. Faced with demands for official protection from its own merchants and investors, Britain tried to defend its main economic interests by leasing the port of Weihaiwei and the Kowloon New Territories adjoining

Hong Kong. It also secured an exclusive railway concession for the Yangtze River valley. Yet the British government still had little interest in acquiring formal control over Chinese territory, and it supported the U.S. open door policy toward commerce in China. As the colonial secretary, Joseph Chamberlain, explained in 1900: "We are not likely ever to want to take possession of any territory in the interior ourselves; but we ought to try for some understanding which will keep off all others."

Although most of the imperial powers formally supported the free trade ideals of the open door policy, the scramble for Chinese concessions continued unabated. By the eve of the First World War, China had lost effective control of almost all of its economically significant coastal regions. Foreign investors controlled one-third of its cotton spinning industries, over three-fourths of its shipping, and almost all of its iron production and railways. Unlike Africa, China was never partitioned politically as a result of being divided into spheres of influence. For the most part, the Chinese retained enough political and social cohesion to withstand foreign threats to their overall sovereignty. Moreover, recognizing that a reasonably unified China was the best protector of its economic interests, Britain worked actively to defend the Ch'ing dynasty from its concession-hunting imperial rivals.

British imperialists actively supported the Chinese government's efforts to modernize its antiquated armed forces by adopting a Western-style economic base. Reform-minded Chinese officials used their influence during the reign of child-emperor T'ung-chih in the 1860s and 1870s to institute a "self-strengthening program" that sought to acquire Western firearms, artillery, and gunboats. They founded a translation institute to gather information on Western economics, political thought, and culture, and broke with China's long-standing xenophobia and isolationism by sending Chinese students and diplomatic missions to study in Europe and the United States. Recognizing that Europe's military supremacy was a product of its industrial base, the reformers also established government-supervised shipping, mining, telegraph, and railway ventures to reduce the influence of foreign investors in China.

Rather than seeing these independent ventures as a threat to their Chinese interests, British merchants and consuls were strong supporters of the reformers. Robert Hart, head of the maritime customs service, wrote, "I want to make China strong, and I want to make England her best friend." Sympathetic British officials helped run China's new arsenals, dockyards, factories, and schools, and they welcomed visiting Chinese missions in metropolitan Britain. Yet the Chinese were careful not to become too dependent on any single source of assistance; they balanced their ties to Britain by employing private technical advisers from almost every major European power.

Although the Chinese managed to develop a small indigenous modern arms industry, they were no more successful than the Asante in emulating the West's economic and military success. Most of China's state-run industrial ventures were undercapitalized, and their products were often inferior and prohibitively expensive. Many foreign technical experts were more concerned with enriching themselves than with providing useful advice to the Chinese. Horatio Lay, the first inspector general of the customs service, was commissioned by the Chinese government to purchase a fleet of eight British-built gunboats in 1862. When Lay and his hand-picked British naval commander claimed jurisdiction over China's entire navy, the Chinese government had little choice but to disband his entire flotilla at a cost of over half a million pounds.

These sorts of fiascoes were expensive and humiliating, but the failure of the self-strengthening program was due primarily, as was the case with the Asante, to opposition from conservative forces within Chinese society. The introduction of Western-style education required reform of the Confucian-based examination system that was the basis of the entire Chinese bureaucracy. Conservatives worried that it would not be possible to acquire modern military technology without also opening China to the divisive influence of Christianity and Western culture. Confident that the foreign imperialists could be safely confined to the coast as long as China maintained its social cohesion, they used popular support to force most of the reformers to resign in disgrace, and in 1908 a reactionary faction of Ch'ing elites recaptured the most influential positions in the imperial court.

Nevertheless, conservatives could not prevent the imperial powers from dividing China into spheres of influence. Frustrated by their inability to halt the erosion of Chinese sovereignty, in 1900 senior Chinese officials rashly lent their support to a secret society known as the Righteous and Harmonious Fists, an organization dedicated to driving all foreigners from China. The leaders of the movement promoted a regimen of special calisthenics that they guaranteed would render their followers invulnerable to bullets. Reactionary Ch'ing officials promised the Boxers, as the society came to be known, a bounty for each foreigner they killed. Most Chinese Christians in Peking were slaughtered during the course of the Boxer Rebellion. European missionaries and diplomats barricaded themselves in their consulates to escape the same fate and waited until a multinational relief force of 18,000 men (one-sixth of which was British) rescued them several months later.

The victorious imperial powers imposed an extremely harsh punitive settlement on the Chinese. In addition to demanding an indemnity of almost £70 million, they forced China to dismantle most of its maritime defenses and imposed a five-year suspension of the prestigious civil service exams in every major city that supported the Boxers. Although the British government took an active role in drafting the terms of China's capitulation, it also used its diplomatic influence to prevent its partners, particularly Russia and Japan, from annexing extensive amounts of Chinese territory. Nevertheless, the humiliation of having foreign troops occupying Peking was more than the Ch'ing dynasty could withstand. In 1911, it was replaced by Sun Yat-sen's shaky republic, which was too weak to prevent China from collapsing into civil war and warlordism.

Britain did not profit directly from the collapse of the Chinese Empire. The anarchy in China's hinterland disrupted trade, threatened foreign investment, and made it harder for Britain to protect its interests through informal methods. Yet it would have been a Herculean task for an outside force to impose order on the turbulent Chinese countryside. British imperialists instead used their military resources and informal influence to maintain a degree of stability in the old treaty ports. The Chinese case clearly demonstrates that political and economic turmoil did not always create opportunities for British imperialism.

BRITISH IMPERIALISM IN THE OTTOMAN EMPIRE

Throughout most of the imperial century, Britain was equally committed to maintaining the territorial integrity and internal stability of the Ottoman Empire. Yet Britain's interests in the world's largest Muslim state were as strategic as they were economic. British merchants had commercial ties to the Middle East dating back to the sixteenth century, but in the nineteenth century the Ottoman Empire's primary value was as a strategic buffer for British links to India. British imperialists wanted

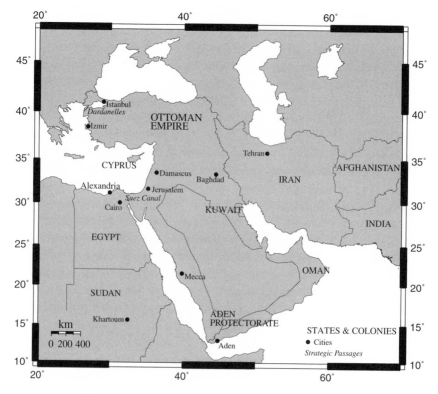

Map 5.2   British Influence in the Middle East, c. 1914

the Ottomans to be strong enough to keep the French and Russians out of the eastern Mediterranean but not strong enough to close the Middle Eastern overland and maritime routes to Asia. Thus, as was the case in China, they supported Ottoman "modernizers" who sought to revitalize the empire through political and economic reform.

Faced with Austrian and Russian expansion in the Balkans, the Ottomans adopted their own version of a self-strengthening program almost a full century before the Chinese. In the late eighteenth century, Sultan Selim III sent diplomatic missions to London and the other major European capitals to secure Western military technology. Yet, as the Chinese were also to discover, it was virtually impossible to emulate Europe's technical achievements without also spreading Western culture.

Islamic intellectuals were wary of the reforms, and Selim was murdered by outraged Janissaries who refused to tolerate the creation of a new, westernized corps of soldiers.

Nevertheless, Sultan Mahmud II, Selim's successor, recognized the desperate need to strengthen the empire's armed forces and orchestrated a massacre of the Janissaries in 1826. He also resumed the quest for Western technology, which had been suspended on Selim's death, by sending student missions to Europe and establishing a translation bureau. These initiatives produced a small faction of Western-oriented bureaucrats and army officers who sought to reinvigorate the empire by strengthening its military, social, and economic institutions. Although they had little popular support, they introduced an era of reform known as the Tanzimat ("reorganization"), which lasted from the 1830s until the 1870s. Having begun their careers in the embassies of Paris and London, these bureaucratic elites received support and encouragement from Britain and other the Western governments with a stake in preserving the Ottoman Empire.

Recognizing that the great powers used the non-Muslim minorities as an excuse to intervene in Ottoman affairs, the reformers sought to create a more socially unified state. By resolving this "Eastern question" they hoped to end foreign interference in their internal affairs. This was a difficult task because the status of the millets was determined by Islamic law, and Muslim clerics strongly criticized the Tanzimat movement. The reformers used Western support to help overcome this conservative opposition but did not abandon their Islamic ideals to espouse Western-style secular nationalism. Midhat Pasha, one of leading architects of the Tanzimat reforms, argued that Islam was representative and democratic. Nevertheless, it was simply impossible to grant non-Muslim minorities the rights of full citizenship in an Islamic state.

The success of the 1829 Greek revolt exposed the growing weakness of the empire. Unable to defeat the Greeks on his own, Mahmud II had to turn to Muhammad Ali for help. As the autonomous governor of Egypt, Muhammad Ali had transformed the Egyptian army into a modern, Western-style force. Egyptian assistance came too late to forestall Greek independence, but in 1831 Muhammad Ali exploited Mahmud's military weakness by invading Syria with the intention of setting himself up as sultan. Lacking the resources to defeat the Egyptian menace on his own, Mahmud appealed to Britain for protection. In return for driving Muhammad Ali out of Syria, the British government pressed the Ottomans to support the Tanzimat reformers. In 1839, the sultan issued the Hatti-Sharif of Gulhane, which guaranteed full rights for the empire's non-Muslim minorities.

Britain hoped these measures would strengthen the Ottoman Empire by reducing the ethnic tensions that had produced the Greek revolt. Lord Palmerston spoke of rejuvenating their "rotten empire" through the introduction of Western-style administrative reforms. Even pro-Ottoman British imperialists believed that the corrupting effects of the harem and oriental despotism had robbed the empire of its martial vigor. Led by Stratford Canning, Britain's ambassador in Istanbul, they considered themselves the Ottomans' tutors. Most British merchants supported these efforts in the hope that the Tanzimat reforms would make it easier to enforce contracts and collect debts.

Yet Britain's strategic goals in the Middle East often conflicted with its economic interests. Although British imperialists tried to help the Ottomans preserve their territorial integrity, they were not willing to allow them to close their markets to British goods. Generally speaking, the Ottoman Empire exported cereals, raw cotton, dyes, silk, and opium and imported finished textiles, iron, and machinery. The British Levant Company, which held a royal monopoly on commerce in the eastern Mediterranean until 1825, captured most of this trade during the Napoleonic Wars as the Royal Navy drove off its continental competitors. When peacetime commerce resumed in the 1830s, Britain's share of the Ottoman market amounted to over 10 percent of the empire's exports and almost 20 percent of its imports.

Although this trade was only a small part of Britain's total international commerce, it had a corrosive effect on the Ottoman Empire. The bulk of British imports were inexpensive cotton goods that undercut Ottoman spinners and weavers. Moreover, European merchants of all nationalities relied on local intermediaries known as dragomans. Like the Chinese comprador, the Ottoman dragoman served as a translator, broker, and intelligence collector. Most shifted their allegiance to their foreign employers because they were usually Jews and Christians with little personal stake in the survival of the Ottoman system. Thus Western commerce had a much greater impact in the Ottoman Empire than it did in China. It damaged indigenous handicraft industries and inflamed existing social divisions.

Recognizing the deleterious effects of unrestricted foreign trade, the Ottoman government tried to assume greater control over its internal economy in the 1820s. It established state monopolies on key commodities and industries in an effort to generate enough revenue to modernize its armed forces. It also restricted the activities of foreign merchants and set strict limits on what they could export. Although British imperialists supported the overall goals of this program, they could not tolerate its means. State monopolies flew in the face of the principles of free trade. The British government insisted on their abolition as a condition of its military support against Muhammad Ali. The 1838 Treaty of Balta Liman forced the Ottomans to dismantle their state monopolies and fix tariffs on foreign imports at just 3 percent. As an Egyptian vassal, Muhammad Ali was also bound by the treaty, and Britain insisted that he disband his own system of Egyptian state monopolies as well.

The British government further undermined the stability of the Ottoman Empire by insisting on extraterritorial protection for its citizens and local allies. Arguing that the Ottoman legal system was "too barbarous" for British subjects, it used the old capitulation agreements to undermine Ottoman sovereignty. Joining with the other great powers, Britain had its consuls sell British passports and protection to their dragomans and Ottoman clients, many of whom were non–Muslims. Although these special privileges served British economic interests, they undermined the Tanzimat reformers by reinforcing the ethnic and communal tensions that divided Ottoman society. British consuls had so much influence by the end of the nineteenth century that even Muslim businessmen sought their aid in resolving commercial disputes.

Britain also used its informal influence to suppress the Middle Eastern slave trade, which amounted to at least 10,000 slaves per year in the 1840s. The British government forced the Ottomans to allow the Royal Navy to search and seize any slaving vessel flying an Ottoman flag. Palmerston was reluctant to interfere so deeply in Ottoman affairs but was pressured into doing so by the abolitionists. British consuls in the Middle East advised him that direct intervention would destabilize the empire because they believed (incorrectly) that slavery was an integral part of Islam. In fact most Ottomans considered domestic slavery a relatively benign institution, since they were ignorant of the horrors of the slave trade, and suspected the British abolitionists of exaggeration.

The ease with which Britain and the other great powers intervened in Ottoman affairs indicates how easy it would have been to partition the empire. Yet very few British imperialists favored such a drastic step. As was the case in China, they were hesitant to assume the responsibility of governing another large non-European population. Russia, on the other hand, had no such reservations. Depicting themselves as the protectors of Orthodox Christians and Slavic peoples in general, Russians invaded Ottoman Romanian provinces in 1854. The British government considered this invasion intolerable because an Ottoman collapse would have given Russia direct access to the eastern Mediterranean. Joining with France, which was equally concerned with maintaining the diplomatic balance of power in Europe, the British government went to war to defend the Ottoman Empire.

Britain's marginal victory over Russia in the Crimean War, which lasted from 1854 to 1856, came at a high price in men and resources. Afterward, the British government sought to strengthen the Ottoman Empire by pressing the sultan to issue the Hatti-Humayun of 1856, which modernized tax collection and reaffirmed the judicial equality of non-Muslims in Ottoman society. Yet these reforms failed to appease Slavic minorities in the Balkans. In 1875, the Russians used a Christian revolt in Bosnia as an excuse to renew their attack on the Ottomans. Faced with the prospect of another Crimean War, the Tanzimat reformers deposed Sultan Abdulaziz and convinced his successor, Abdulhamid, to accept a limited constitution.

The British government supported these reforms and used the threat of war to keep the Russians from dismantling the empire. It did not, however, prevent the great powers from recognizing most of the Ottoman Balkan territories as independent states at the 1878 Congress of Berlin. Moreover, Abdulhamid ended the Tanzimat period that same year by disbanding the first Ottoman parliament and freezing the constitution of 1876. The steady loss of Ottoman territory in the Balkans removed the incentive to accommodate his Christian subjects, and Abdulhamid sought to strengthen his hold on the remaining Islamic heartland by emphasizing his titular role as the worldwide leader of the Muslim community.

British politicians blamed the Ottomans' weakness on their inability to implement modern reforms, but in reality British economic interests in the Ottoman Empire undermined the goals of the Tanzimat program substantially. Until the Crimean War, the Ottomans had wisely refrained from borrowing large sums of money to fund their modernization efforts. Recognizing that heavy national debts led to dependency, Sultan Abdulmecid had ordered his grand viziers to repudiate several unauthorized foreign loans despite the heavy penalties that came from early cancellation. The Crimean War, however, forced the Ottomans to borrow extensively from Britain and France on extremely unfavorable terms. They borrowed 241,900,000 Turkish lira between 1854 and 1874, but only received 127,570,000 Turkish lira after the London financial houses, which raised the loans, deducted their expenses and commissions. Although the bulk of these funds originally went to the war and the Tanzimat reforms, by the 1870s the Ottomans had to borrow extensively just to keep up their interest payments.

Faced with the burden of a mounting national debt, the Ottomans defaulted on their loans in 1876 and declared formal bankruptcy three years later. Their European creditors refused to accept these tactics and attended the Congress of Berlin to demand protection for their investments. Even though British bondholders held less than 15 percent of the Ottoman public debt (the French held 60 percent), the British government was unwilling to allow the Ottomans to disrupt the growing international network of credit and finance. In 1879 it sent warships of the Royal Navy into the eastern Mediterranean to remind them of their fiscal responsibilities.

More significantly, three years later Britain joined with France in forming the Ottoman Public Debt Commission to manage the empire's finances. Led by a seven-member council representing the major European creditors, the commission assumed control of the empire's taxes and tariffs on salt, stamps, spirits, fish, tobacco, and silk, as well as the tribute of several major provinces, to fund the Ottomans' national debt. From 1881 to 1914 it appropriated approximately a quarter of all government revenues. With a staff of almost 10,000 employees on the eve of the First World War, the commission undermined Ottoman sovereignty severely by capturing the most viable sectors of their economy.

The British government therefore began to reconsider its support for the Ottomans as the empire grew markedly weaker in the final decades of the imperial century. In 1878 Britain annexed Cyprus, abandoning its long-standing reluctance to acquire Ottoman territory. The island itself had little inherent value, but its strategic location in the eastern Mediterranean allowed Britain to close the Dardanelles to the Russian navy in time of war. Moreover, the opening of the Suez Canal in 1869 shortened the passage to India markedly and shifted Britain's strategic focus in the Middle East from defending Turkey and the Dardanelles to ensuring that Egypt remained open to British commerce and influence.

British imperialists therefore began to take a much greater interest in Egyptian affairs. Although the heirs of Muhammad Ali remained nominal vassals of the Ottoman sultan, by midcentury they secured the hereditary right to rule Egypt as autonomous Khedives (a Persian title meaning lord or master). In the 1860s the Khedive Ismail presided over an economic boom driven primarily by rising cotton prices brought on by the U.S. Civil War. Ismail continued his grandfather's efforts to reform Egypt along Western lines: "My country is no longer in Africa, it is in Europe." Ismail borrowed heavily on future cotton earnings to introduce Western technology and amenities to Egypt but was caught off-guard when global cotton prices dropped when peace returned to the United States. By the 1870s Ismail was so deeply in debt that, as was the case with his Ottoman suzerain, he had to borrow continuously just to pay the interest on his previous loans.

Ismail's growing insolvency allowed Britain to acquire considerable influence in Egyptian internal affairs. In 1875, Prime Minister Benjamin Disraeli purchased the Egyptian government's 44 percent share of the Suez Canal for just £4 million. The purchase made sense from a strategic point of view because 80 percent of canal traffic in the 1870s was British. When Ismail finally defaulted on his loans in 1876, the British government joined with his other European creditors in forming a debt commission to take control of Egypt's economic affairs. They diverted revenues from state railways, telegraphs, and customs receipts, as well as taxes from four provinces (which amounted to almost sixty percent of the national budget in 1880), to service the Egyptian national debt of almost £100 million. In addition to managing Egypt's finances, Europeans also organized and ran its cotton trade, banking sector, and telegraph and postal systems. By 1881, there were over 90,000 foreigners living in Egypt, most of whom enjoyed extraterritorial legal protection under the Ottoman capitulation treaties.

Most Egyptians naturally resented this increased foreign interference in their internal affairs. Ismail himself was deposed by his European creditors (who acted with the tacit assent of Sultan Abdulhamid) for the crime of trying to regain control of his finances in 1879. His son Tewfiq had considerable difficulty containing the growing hostility of native-born Egyptians, who considered the Turkish-speaking Khedives foreigners, toward his government and the restrictive policies of the debt commission he was bound to uphold. In 1882, Col. Urabi Pasha led middle-ranking Egyptian army officers in a popular revolt that forced Tewfiq to accept a council of nationalist Egyptian ministers.

Faced with the prospect that the new regime might repudiate its financial responsibilities, British bondholders, who held the majority of the Egyptian debt, lobbied their government for protection. British politicians of both parties usually refused to use state resources to support private economic interests, but Prime Minister William Gladstone made an exception in Egypt. Fearing that French investors would acquire too much influence in Egypt if he equivocated, the Liberal prime minister sent the Royal Navy to the Egyptian port of Alexandria to demonstrate Britain's resolve. Yet Gladstone did not intend to add Egypt to Britain's formal empire. He had originally hoped to work in cooperation with the French, who were the Egyptians' other main creditors, but was forced to act alone when the French Chamber of Deputies refused to take part in the operation. Gladstone's primary goal was to strengthen Britain's informal influence in Egypt through the threat of military intervention.

Nevertheless, Britain found itself in the difficult position of having to occupy Egypt in the summer of 1882. Although the British government denied that it had imperial designs on Egypt, its local representatives appeared to have other ideas. The commander of the Royal Navy flotilla ignited a wave of bloody antiforeign riots in Alexandria by opening fire on the city after its shore batteries refused his demands to surrender. Claiming to be the protector of Tewfiq and the Suez Canal, Britain landed an expeditionary force to restore order and expel Urabi Pasha from the Egyptian government. Yet the canal was never in much danger. It was over a hundred miles from Alexandria and was never threatened by Urabi and the nationalists. In hindsight, it appears that the canal and the riots provided the British government with a justification to intervene on behalf of British bondholders.

Gladstone declared that the British occupation was a temporary measure intended only to reestablish financial responsibility in Egypt. Yet he could not follow through on the promise to withdraw from Egypt because outraged French officials blocked his attempt to secure international recognition for Britain's informal role as the primary tutor and sponsor of the Egyptian government. More importantly, no British politician was willing to surrender the strategically important Suez Canal. Thus the British grudgingly assumed greater responsibility for governing Egypt.

This commitment also forced Britain to extend its influence into the Sudan. The British government had previously been content to leave the territory in the hands of Muhammad Ahmed, commonly known as the Mahdi, even though in 1885 he had massacred famous British general Sir Charles Gordon (who rose to fame defending Shanghai from the Taipings) along with the Egyptian garrison of Khartoum. Yet, as the unofficial rulers of Egypt, British officials were forced to reoccupy the region in the late 1890s to prevent France and their other imperial rivals from controlling the upper reaches of the Nile.

In governing Egypt, Britain preserved the Khedival administration to reduce costs and avoid provoking the nation's other European creditors. Tewfiq and his ministers retained their nominal authority but were now responsible to the British consul-general. Each Egyptian government ministry was run by a British adviser, and by the turn of the century, there were over 1,000 generously paid British civil servants in the country. Britain administered the Sudan, which was technically an Egyptian colony, through a cadre of British advisers and a bureaucracy paid for and staffed by the Egyptian government. Egypt itself remained an autonomous province of the Ottoman Empire until the eve of the First World War but essentially became an informal British protectorate.

The failure of the Tanzimat reforms allowed British imperialists to justify these blatant infringements of Ottoman sovereignty on moralistic grounds. Adbulhamid's suspension of the constitution of 1876 and his brutal methods in suppressing a Christian uprising in Bulgaria in the 1880s angered humanitarians in Britain. Arguing in favor of a moral basis for British foreign policy, Gladstone branded the Ottomans inhumane oppressors of non-Muslim minorities. The International Anti-Slavery Society, incensed by the continued toleration of slavery in the empire, issued its "Address to Electors of Great Britain" during the elections of 1880, which pressed politicians of both parties to revise their pro-Ottoman foreign policies. Although Palmerston and Canning styled themselves as "tutors" of the Tanzimat reformers, their successors considered

Abdulhamid an illiberal Asian despot who trampled on the personal free-
doms of his subjects.

Britain's declining economic interests in the eastern Mediterranean
also made it relatively easy for British imperialists to abandon the Ottomans. In 1880 45 percent of the Ottomans' imports came from Britain,
but in the first decade of the twentieth century British manufacturers
supplied less than a quarter of the empire's imports. Overall, the Ottomans accounted for less than 2 percent of Britain's overseas exports during this period. A community of British speculators held a substantial
stake in the production of dyes, raw cotton, grapes, and opium around
the Turkish port of Izmir, and India-based shippers and traders had extensive interests in the Persian Gulf. Yet, for the most part, British investors generally avoided the Ottoman Empire. Put off by the empire's de-
fault in 1876, London financiers had sold most of their Ottoman
holdings to French and German concerns by the turn of the century.
The British government tried to preserve its influence in the eastern
Mediterranean and the Middle East by lending unofficial support to the
National Bank of Turkey, but the bank failed in 1913 when British investors refused to risk their money in the Ottoman Empire.

Anglo-Ottoman relations declined even further after the revolt of
the Young Turks in 1908. They forced Abdulhamid to restore the 1876
constitution and then replaced him one year later with his younger
brother, who was little more than a figurehead. The Young Turks were
primarily young army officers and political refugees who imbibed the
lessons of revolutionary nationalism during exile in the major capitals of
Europe. Their goal was to prevent the further dismemberment of the
empire, particularly in the Balkans, through a renewed program of political and military reform. Unlike their Tanzimat predecessors, however,
they did so by emphasizing secular (which in practice meant Turkish)
nationalism over the Pan-Islamicism of Abdulhamid. Their Committee
of Union and Progress, which governed the empire during the final
years of the imperial century, suppressed all alternative political associa-
tions based on ethnic or religious identities, essentially spelling the end
of the millet system. The seemingly endless series of revolts and uprisings
in the Balkans demonstrated that there was little possibility of winning
the allegiance of the empire's remaining non-Muslim minorities.

At first glance, it might have appeared that Britain would have welcomed the Young Turks' efforts to strengthen what was left of the em-

pire. Yet this was not the case. With the acquisition of Egypt, British imperialists no longer felt the need to defend the routes to India by propping up the Ottomans. On the contrary, both Abdulhamid and the Committee of Union and Progress endangered British interests in the Middle East by forming close relations with Germany. British imperialists saw German plans for a Berlin-to-Baghdad railway as a threat to their influence in the Persian Gulf and, by extension, the security of India. It therefore became more practical for the British government to ally itself with Russia, an Ottoman foe of long standing, than to continue to support the territorial integrity of the empire. This Anglo-Russian entente, coupled with British meddling in Arabia, brought the Young Turks into the First World War on the side of the Germans. As a result, Britain willingly participated in the final dissolution of the Ottoman Empire after the Central Powers were defeated in 1918.

Although the Ottoman and Chinese Empires eventually collapsed under the weight of their own internal problems, they managed to preserve their sovereignty throughout the imperial century. Their success was due in part to Britain's commitment to maintaining their territorial integrity. Rather than resort to the expense of partition, British imperialists used their informal influence, backed by military force when necessary, to push the Ottomans and Chinese into instituting economic and social reforms that served Britain's economic and strategic interests.

For the most part, the British government refused to acquire large sections of Ottoman and Chinese territory. Using its advantages judiciously, it annexed Hong Kong and Cyprus to achieve specific economic and strategic goals; it assumed control of Egypt only after it became an autonomous Ottoman province. This self-restraint was due primarily to the realization that the Chinese and Ottoman Empires were more valuable intact. The Chinese government maintained a relatively favorable environment for foreign commerce and investment, and the Ottoman Empire was a useful strategic buffer against Britain's imperial rivals.

It is important to note that Britain's self-restraint in China and the Middle East was also due to the relative cohesion of Chinese and Ottoman society. Although the compradors and dragomans aligned themselves with European imperialists, they were culturally isolated and had little overall influence in their host societies. In China the scope and influence of Christian missionaries was limited by cultural self-confidence and general xenophobia, and in the Ottoman Empire by the viability of

Islam. Western missions in China had to offer cash rewards to win converts, and missionary evangelists in the Middle East made little headway among Jewish and Orthodox Christian Ottoman subjects. Unlike the Indians and Africans, the Chinese and Ottomans avoided becoming subjects of the British Empire because their cohesiveness rendered Britain's system of indirect rule largely unworkable. Without local allies to serve as colonial intermediaries, Britain would have had to occupy and hold Ottoman and Chinese territory by military force. Thus British imperialists found it cheaper and more practical to work through existing political and economic institutions.

SUGGESTIONS FOR FURTHER READING

Dean, Britten. "British Informal Empire: The Case of China." *Journal of Commonwealth and Comparative Politics* 14 (1976): 64–81.

Galbraith, John, and Afaf Lufti Al-Sayyid-Marsot. "The British Occupation of Egypt: Another View." *International Journal of Middle East Studies* 9 (1978): 471–488.

Hopkins, A .G. "The Victorians and Africa: A Reconsideration of the Occupation of Egypt, 1882." *Journal of African History* 27 (1986): 363–391.

Hsu, Immanuel C.Y. *The Rise of Modern China*. 5th ed. New York: Oxford University Press, 1995.

Lewis, Bernard. *The Emergence of Modern Turkey*. 2d ed. New York: Oxford University Press, 1968.

Mitchell, Timothy. *Colonising Egypt*. Cambridge: Cambridge University Press, 1988.

Murphy, Rhoads. *The Outsiders: The Western Experience in India and China*. Ann Arbor: University of Michigan Press, 1977.

Toledano, Ehud. *The Ottoman Slave Trade and Its Suppression, 1840–1890*. Princeton: Princeton University Press, 1983.

6

THE CONSEQUENCES OF EMPIRE

Having explored the expansion of Britain's formal and informal empire over the course of the imperial century, we shall now examine the consequences of imperialism for both the subject peoples of the empire and the British themselves. Even though Britain never integrated its far-flung possessions into a single administrative unit, the British Empire accelerated the historical process of globalization by breaking down geographic, political, and economic barriers throughout the world. British rule and informal influence precipitated this process of globalization by joining diverse regions and peoples on every continent (save Antarctica) into a vast global commercial and financial network.

Given the decentralized nature of the empire, as well as Britain's preference for indirect rule and informal influence, the most common point of reference for a Maasai pastoralist, an Egyptian peasant, an Indian sepoy, and a Chinese comprador were British culture and the economic demands of British imperialism. Subject peoples of the empire often suffered considerable hardship when British imperialists sought to restructure their societies to serve specific economic ends. But, as has been shown in previous chapters, British imperialism was viable only when it convinced a sufficient segment of the local population to participate in the imperial enterprise. Although an influential coalition of British merchants, industrialists, administrators, and settlers benefited from the evolution of the British Empire into a global institution, their control of this vast, multiethnic conglomeration of territories was never total or absolute.

Therefore the expansion of Britain's formal rule and informal influence had a number of unforeseen consequences. Many older histories of the British Empire have focused exclusively on the intentional one-way transfer of British political and cultural norms to the colonies. But in reality, Britain's jury-rigged institutions of imperial rule and influence created an interconnecting network that dispersed subject populations and cultures to every corner of the empire, including Britain itself. By uniting disparate regions of the world under a series of overlapping but largely decentralized administrative systems, British imperialism diffused a diverse array of peoples, cultures, flora, and fauna around the globe.

The legacy of this process of demographic, cultural, and biological cross-pollination is decidedly mixed. British rule facilitated the exchange of new ideas and useful products among the peoples of the empire, but it also touched off deadly epidemics in formerly isolated populations by exposing them to infectious diseases. Moreover, Britain's technological and military superiority sparked a profound crisis of confidence among its non-Western subjects, which left these peoples ill-equipped to resist the intrusion of foreign customs and values. In recent years, historians have paid close attention to the efforts of British administrators to impose Western cultural values on their colonial subjects. Yet language, religion, law, and education are ambiguous institutions that can never be fully possessed or controlled by any single government or ruling class. Colonial peoples frequently used Britain's own cultural values to resist or temper the impact of British imperialism, in addition to preserving key elements of their social institutions that served the same purpose.

Furthermore, British imperialists themselves played an active but largely unthinking role in reinforcing and disseminating the cultures of their subjects by incorporating non-Western institutions into the system of indirect rule. To be sure, Protestant Christianity, British law, and the English language were the dominant cultural institutions of the empire, but British administrators had to understand and co-opt the customs of their subjects in order to govern them. These officials were often profoundly influenced by this process, and many continued to indulge in non-Western languages, dress, cuisine, and sometimes even religion after they returned home to Britain. Moreover, a small handful of Asians and Africans took advantage of their status as British subjects to work and study in Great Britain itself. Thus the British population became increasingly aware that they were part of a vast multiethnic empire over the course of the imperial century. Proponents of imperialism sought to win support for their cause by nurturing these sentiments in British schools and by celebrating Britain's imperial glories in the music halls and in popular fiction.

Yet the influence of non-Westerners on the form and character of the empire went far beyond broadening the horizons of the British public. British colonial officials had to govern as Indian, African, and Asian rulers to establish their legitimacy and avoid provoking widespread unrest. Moreover, they often transplanted these administrative systems and other useful cultural institutions from one territory to another. This was particularly true in regard to India, which exerted the greatest influence on the British Empire by virtue of its status as the oldest, largest, and most economically important of Britain's non-Western colonies. British imperialists perfected the system of indirect rule in India and exported it to most of their African colonies. Similarly, Indian merchants, soldiers, policemen, and laborers could be found in virtually ever corner of the empire by the end of the imperial century. To a lesser degree, British imperialism also diffused African and Asian peoples and cultures in a similar manner.

Thus the expansion of Britain's formal empire and informal influence produced a hybrid culture that was British in appearance but not entirely British in substance. The legacy of this imperial culture lives on in the English-speaking former colonies that continue to use British models as the basis of their educational and legal systems, as well as in the increasingly multicultural nature of metropolitan Britain itself.

BRITISH INFLUENCES ON THE EMPIRE

The spread of the English language and British culture strengthened Britain's hold on its formal possessions and greatly enhanced its informal influence throughout the globe. Just as Latin and the social and material culture of Rome were the cornerstones of the Roman Empire, British cultural institutions were the glue holding together the disparate peoples and territories of the British Empire. Informal influence and indirect rule were pragmatic and economical ways of reordering and governing non-Western populations, but the small handful of British merchants, missionaries, settlers, and administrators took care not be absorbed into the colonized majority. Lacking a centralized system of imperial rule, British imperialists stridently defended their cultural autonomy in an effort to maintain both their identity and their authority.

Although the Indian Mutiny appeared to illustrate the dangers of meddling too deeply in non-Western societies, the British Empire ultimately depended on a class of westernized translators, commercial agents, and clerks to mediate between the British ruling classes and the general population. Even though the ideology of indirect rule committed British administrators to respect the cultural autonomy of their non-Western subjects, in reality, Africans and Asians had to assimilate British values and customs to achieve a measure of social and political advancement in most colonial societies.

Interestingly enough, the entrenchment of British culture in Africa and Asia was rarely driven by direct British settlement. As was noted in chapter 1, Malthusian fears of overpopulation in Great Britain were one of the primary factors behind the expansion of British imperialism in the nineteenth century. As the British population quadrupled between 1801 and 1901, over 20 million people emigrated from the British Isles. Driven by the enclosure of communal land in the countryside, the decline of older handicraft industries, low wages, urban unemployment, and the Irish Famine, most emigrants settled in the United States and the English-speaking settler colonies that were vestiges of Britain's first overseas empire. Thus the wave of nineteenth-century British emigration, which rivaled the African slave trade in sheer numbers, had little impact on tropical regions of the world.

The British government rarely played a role in determining where its citizens ultimately settled. Most emigrants left Britain voluntarily, but the government also forcibly deported large numbers of convicts to Australia. India attracted only a handful of British planters, and less than 5 percent of all British settlers landed in eastern and southern Africa. In the 1820s the British government supported British immigration in South Africa to balance the Afrikaners; later in the nineteenth century it promoted the British settlement of the East Africa Protectorate (Kenya) to provide paying customers for the Uganda railway. Yet most Britons emigrated without the official support of their government and therefore chose to settle in North America, Australia, or New Zealand, which had neither an unhealthy tropical climate nor an entrenched non-Western population.

British emigrants rarely settled in territories under the control of a foreign power (with the exception of the United States), but when they did they sought to preserve their cultural identity. The British community in Argentina maintained its own churches, newspapers, and clubs, and sent its children to be educated in Britain. There are only a handful of cases in which British emigrants, who were usually Scottish, Welsh, or Irish, were assimilated into a non-English-speaking majority. In the early nineteenth century, a group of Irish immigrants merged with the Afrikaner community of the Cape Colony, and in Argentina a settlement of Scottish Catholics adopted the culture of the Spanish-speaking majority. Yet both the Argentines and the Afrikaners were of European descent, and there are no recorded instances of significant numbers of British emigrants being absorbed into a non-Western society.

The impact of British emigration on non-Western peoples was largely determined by the size of their population, the complexity of their political institutions, their ability to resist British colonists by force of arms, and the extent of their biological resistance to contagious disease. The peoples of Africa and Asia were fortunate to live in tropical regions that were unsuitable for large-scale European settlement, and most had the social and political capacity to survive the imperial century. On the other hand, the indigenous inhabitants of North America and Australia were largely wiped out by the disease, warfare, and economic disruption generated by their encounter with European imperialism. This grim process of extermination began in the sixteenth and seventeenth centuries and was carried to its grim conclusion over the course of the nineteenth century.

Most Australian Aborigines were still using stone tools and subsisting by hunting and gathering when they first encountered British explorer James Cook in 1770. With no common language and no form of political organization larger than a clan of interrelated family groups, they were ill equipped to prevent Britain from turning their country into a penal colony. Amerindians such as the Huron residents of what is today the Canadian province of Ontario and the Nookta of Vancouver Island lived in more complex agricultural societies, but they too lacked the political and military capacity to turn back the tide of European settlement. More significantly, the geographic isolation of both Aborigines and Amerindians meant that both groups had little natural resistance to the Old World diseases that imperialism introduced into Australia and North

America. As a result, vast numbers died of measles, smallpox, typhus, and typhoid.

Earlier generations of imperial historians preferred to depict Australia and North America as relatively empty, but in reality the creation of settlement colonies almost always entailed the subjugation and eventual extermination of the original inhabitants of these regions. Although Britain did not intentionally infect its Australian and North American subjects with lethal pathogens, British imperialists had few reservations about taking advantage of the widespread epidemics caused by the creation of their global empire. Moreover, the appropriation of extensive tracts of land for cities and settler farms further weakened indigenous societies by depriving Aborigines and Amerindians of the ability to feed themselves. As a result, the Aboriginal population of Australia dropped from approximately 300,000 people in the late eighteenth century to just 80,000 by the 1880s; the 4,000 Aborigines who lived on the southern island of Tasmania were wiped out entirely during the same period. Local colonial officials justified this implicit genocide by using the ideology of "natural law" and Social Darwinism to explain the disappearance of a "backward" people.

For the most part, British imperialists tended to treat the remnants of these doomed societies as pests that had to be either removed to reservations or assimilated into the dominant colonial culture. Most of the survivors of the destruction of Aboriginal society migrated to the slums of Australia's growing cities and fell victim to the urban vices of prostitution, alcoholism, and despair. Settlers' confiscation of hunting and grazing land in British North America caused many vulnerable groups like the Beothuk of Newfoundland to die out entirely. The Canadian government tried to assimilate the survivors through Christian evangelism and vocational training, but even westernized Amerindians were denied voting rights by individual provinces. Humanitarians in both Britain and the colonies tried to temper the most destructive aspects of British emigration in Australia and North America, but most settlers believed that these indigenous peoples were doomed to extinction because they were incapable of surviving in the modern world.

The Maori of New Zealand, however, exposed the fallacy of these bogus arguments. Unlike the Aborigines, the Maori were of Polynesian descent and were comparatively recent immigrants, having settled New Zealand's two islands approximately a thousand years ago. Forced to subsist primarily on sweet potatoes, they developed a highly militaristic culture as rival tribes, or *imi,* competed to control the more temperate regions of the islands in which the potatoes could be grown. In 1642 Dutch explorer Abel Tasman found the Maori living in fortified strategic villages known as *pas,* but he was unable to land because they were openly hostile to foreigners. Although the Maori acquired a reputation for savagery over the next two centuries by attacking subsequent parties of European explorers, they were willing to trade food for iron products and other manufactured goods. Maori men also served as sailors on European whaling and merchant ships and were a common sight in Australian port cities by the beginning of the nineteenth century.

Although they were vulnerable to Old World diseases, the Maori were substantially better equipped to cope with the full onslaught of European settlers during the imperial century. They developed relatively good relations with Britain after the visits of Captain James Cook to the islands in the late eighteenth century, and they valued the technology, agricultural expertise, and literacy that the British had to offer. Even as missionaries made dangerous inroads into Maori society, Maori farmers turned a handsome profit by trading with the Australian colonies. Moreover, the willingness of British merchants to supply firearms to cooperative chiefs altered the balance of power in New Zealand substantially. By the 1830s many Maori had willingly embraced a monetarized economy in addition to adopting Western clothing and customs.

Yet the Maori could not escape the inevitable political crisis and social dislocation that came with increased British settlement in the 1840s. Some Maori made the best of the situation by selling the same tract of land to several different buyers, but the Maori rapidly lost control of the situation. Their attempts to limit the sale of land to foreigners drove them to war with Britain within two decades. The combination of increased warfare among the Maori themselves resulting from the introduction of firearms, the fighting with the British, and the introduction of Old World contagious diseases caused the Maori population, which was approximately 200,000 before the era of colonization, to be reduced by half over the course of the nineteenth century. Nevertheless, the Maori still controlled large sections of the North Island in the 1870s, and their greater ability to adapt to the onslaught of Western culture and settlement allowed them to escape the fate of most of the indigenous societies of Australia and North America that disappeared over the course of the imperial century.

By comparison, India and most of the African colonies acquired by Britain under the "new" imperialism held little appeal for British settlers. The small enclaves of British officials, merchants, and missionaries in these territories therefore had few common points of reference with the non-Western majority. To avoid the necessity of "going native," a derogatory term for a Briton who had surrendered his culture, they developed elaborate customs and traditions to distinguish themselves from their subjects. Many of these colonial social institutions were based on the culture of the landed British gentry, a class that was on the decline in late-nineteenth-century Britain. Nevertheless, exclusive social clubs, Masonic lodges, race tracks, golf courses, and elaborate dining rituals all created the image that every Briton in the colonies was a gentleman and thus was superior to, and separate from, the African and Asian majority.

British imperialists reinforced these social distinctions by either restructuring existing African and Asian cities or creating entirely new urban centers in their colonies. The design of these cities reinforced social divisions between the British and their non-Western subjects. In most British colonies, Europeans settled in segregated neighborhoods that were demarcated by walls, major roads and railway lines, or urban parks. They often lived in unique residences known as bungalows that were built to promote the free flow of air in humid tropical regions. With their high walls, fortified gates, and extensive lawns, these buildings were also intended to isolate European families from the non-Western population of the colonies.

Taken as a whole, these institutions distinguished British imperialists from the colonial majority, thereby providing the legitimacy and moral certainty that established their political authority. Given the importance of segregation to the imperial system, colonial officials were extremely distrustful of any practice or institution that eroded the social distance between themselves and their non-Western subjects. Social interaction, particularly sexual relations, blurred the necessary distinction between the colonizer and the colonized.

Initially, these concerns were less of a factor in eighteenth-century India; company officials behaved as Indian rulers and interacted freely with the Indian population. Since the British East India Company's European staff was almost exclusively male, it was not unusual for British arrivals to take an Indian mistress. These women were often referred to as "sleeping dictionaries" because they supposedly helped their lovers master local languages. The BEIC even offered a five-rupee "christening present" for every half-caste child on the assumption that the boys would become soldiers in the Company's armed forces. As a result, there were at least 10,000 Anglo-Indians at the beginning of the imperial century.

This mixed population played a useful intermediary role during the era of company rule, but its ambiguous status undermined British social distance after the BEIC lost its economic role in the early nineteenth century. In the 1790s, Governor-General Richard Wellesley strongly discouraged company employees from taking Indian mistresses and discharged all Anglo-Indian soldiers. Backed by missionaries who considered sexual relations with Indians immoral, company officials now deemed the half-caste community incompatible with indirect rule. In the Company's eyes, Eurasians were unsuitable political partners because they were allegedly despised by the greater Indian population. Arguing that Anglo-Indians embodied the combined vices of the British and Indian "races," company officials sought to preserve the racial and cultural exclusivity that was the basis of their legitimacy.

The opening of the Suez Canal in 1869 further widened the social distance between Britons and Indians by making it easier for British women to make annual visits to India in search of husbands among the administrative and officer classes. This "fishing fleet," as it was commonly known, reinforced upper-class social etiquette in the British community and conclusively ended the Raj's continued informal tolerance of Indian mistresses and half-caste children. Moreover, the presence of large numbers of British women provided British officials with a further excuse to insist on strict social segregation. Based on the false reports of mass rapes during the Indian Mutiny, popular stereotypes under the Raj depicted Indian men as too sensual and lascivious to be trusted in the company of British women and children. Needless to say, Indian men who established sexual relationships with British women were usually charged with rape. Most educated Indians recognized that these social taboos reinforced their subordinate status, and several Indian princes created severe headaches for their British minders by marrying lower-class European women. Although British officials could not legally prevent these unions, the Raj often barred specific princes from visiting Britain on the suspicion that they were looking for a British wife.

Yet the formal ban on sexual contact with non-Europeans in India did not immediately apply to Britain's new African colonies. In the later decades of the nineteenth century, it was not unusual for colonial administrators to take an African mistress when assigned to a remote rural post. Although the British government officially discouraged the practice, its defenders argued that "native concubines" provided necessary sexual release for junior officials who could not afford to marry. African mistresses were a common fixture in many administrative headquarters and military bases until 1908, when a public clash in the East Africa Protectorate between a district commissioner and an African policeman over an African woman embarrassed senior colonial officials in London. The Colonial Office therefore issued a circular banning interracial sexual relations, declaring that "it is not possible for any member of the administration to countenance such practices without lowering himself in the eyes of the natives" and threatening transgressors with "disgrace and official ruin" for ignoring the ban. Although these official sanctions and informal social taboos prevented members of the colonial administration from publicly acknowledging their mistresses, in reality many British males continued to pursue covert sexual liaisons with non-Western women.

Moreover, it was neither possible nor desirable to erect impermeable social barriers between British imperialists and their colonial subjects. As was pointed out in previous chapters, British imperialism needed allies among the local population. In most cases, British merchants, missionaries, and administrators encouraged the creation of this comprador class by using Western culture to exploit economic and social divisions in African and Asian societies. Furthermore, by fixing the values and traditions of the British gentry as symbols of status, authority, and political legitimacy, imperial officials made the adoption of British culture the key to political and social advancement in colonial society. As seen in previous chapters, educated Africans and Asians often adopted the dress, manners, and traditions of British gentlemen to challenge racial segregation and claim the full rights of British citizenship.

Although Britain's economic and technological accomplishments offered tangible incentives to cooperate with the imperial enterprise, evangelical Protestant Christianity was largely responsible for creating this new class of westernized elites. In addition to providing a legitimiz-

ing ideology for imperialism, the evangelical movement helped undermine the self-confidence of subject peoples by introducing new codes
of ethics, morality, and social behavior. By imbibing these alien values,
non-Western Christians often became alienated from their own cultural
heritage, which in turn weakened the social and political cohesion their
rulers needed to retain their sovereignty in the face of British imperial
expansion.

In addition to spreading Western cultural values, the evangelical
movement also played an important role in transforming British imperialism into a viable governing system. Through their virtual monopoly
on imperial education and medicine, the missions successfully linked
Christianity with economic and social advancement in the colonies. By
serving as teachers and doctors, missionaries offered converts access to
the technological achievements of industrial Europe. Although the doctrine of indirect rule required British officials to recruit non-Christian
"traditional" elites as chiefs and headmen, educated mission converts
monopolized prestigious and high-paying intermediary roles in most
British territories. The majority of the westernized Africans and Asians
who served as commercial agents, translators, and clerks were Christians.
These educated elites received considerable political and economic rewards as compensation for the severe social alienation that came with
their new role.

The ability of a particular society to resist the spread of European
imperialism can be at least partially attributed to the degree to which it
limited the influence of Christian missionaries. Certainly the strength of
Islam in the Ottoman Empire and of Chinese Confucianism drastically
reduced the influence of Western missions, which in return limited the
ability of British imperialists to find allies among the general population.
The decision of African and Asian societies to either reject or embrace
the cultural values of evangelical Christianity was based on a series of
interrelated factors, including ethnic homogeneity, social cohesiveness,
technological accomplishments, and the strength of their own religious
values. Although in a few cases ruling elites embraced Christianity, missionaries tended to have the greatest success converting ethnic or religious minorities, commercially ambitious merchants, and disadvantaged
social classes.

As was pointed out in chapter 2, missionaries did not have much
influence in India until the British East India Company relaxed its re-

striction on Christian evangelism in the early nineteenth century. Although upwardly mobile Hindu and Muslim intellectuals welcomed the opportunities offered by Western education, few were willing to embrace Christianity. British missionaries had the greatest success converting the untouchables and other members of the lower Hindu castes. Seeking access to Western education, famine relief, enhanced social status, and political patronage, entire families and villages converted en masse. As a result, there were approximately 7 million Indian Christians by the close of the imperial century.

The few Muslims and high-caste Hindus to accept Christianity usually did so as students in mission schools. They inevitably faced intense social and economic pressure from their peers and families to renounce their new faith, some even requiring police protection to defend them from physical assaults by outraged ex-coreligionists. Yet, for the most part, Christian conversion was confined largely to India's lower classes. Under the system of indirect rule, Islam and Hinduism remained viable sources of status and political influence for Indian elites. Although the British conquest discredited Mughal and Maratha political institutions, these great non-Western religions were sufficiently well established to resist the pressures of evangelical Christianity. The missionaries actually helped spark a Hindu revival, and in 1843 Hindu mobs rioted in Madras to protest the Church of Scotland Mission's activities in the city. Even though the greater Indian population was unwilling to convert to Christianity, mission schools helped produce the educated intermediary classes that played a vital role in maintaining British rule in India.

In comparison, most African societies found it much harder to limit the divisive impact of Western missionaries. African religions were every bit as vital and dynamic as Hinduism and Islam, but they lacked the scope and written scriptures to withstand the pressures of evangelical Christianity. On the coast of West and East Africa, Islam had already been in the process of transforming indigenous African systems of belief for several centuries. Moreover, the string of military disasters, epidemics, and famines that accompanied the partition of the continent in the nineteenth century caused many Africans to question the validity of their religious convictions. Most African societies retained a belief in a supreme deity, but the colonial conquest shook their faith in the pantheon of spirits and lesser deities that regulated the rhythms of daily life. The old order appeared to be collapsing around them, and Christianity helped Africans adapt to the colonial system and offered access to wealth, education, and medical care.

Africans, nevertheless, did not entirely abandon their cultural values when they converted to Christianity. As in the case of Western education in India, British customs could be an effective means of organizing resistance to imperialism in addition to being instruments of social control. African converts reformulated Christian dogma to suit their own worldview, and in many societies they associated their supreme deity with the God of the Bible. More significantly, the Afro-Victorians founded independent African churches to break the monopoly of Western missions on education and evangelism. Along with the doctrine of Ethiopianism, which established an explicitly African conception of Christianity, these churches were a direct challenge to the ideological bases of imperialism.

The contested nature of Christianity in the empire illustrates the contradictory nature of Britain's cultural influence on its colonies. Even as British imperialists tried to segregate themselves physically and culturally from their non-Western subjects, they tried to use British cultural institutions to expand their influence in African and Asian societies. As noted in previous chapters, British imperialists sought to strengthen their control over India and South Africa by imposing the English language on Indians and Afrikaners in the early nineteenth century. Yet British intellectuals jealously resisted Indian attempts to adapt the language to local circumstances by ridiculing the "babu English" used by members of India's educated classes. In the end, Britain's effort to Anglicize its colonial subjects was a dismal failure. But the extensive use of English today by Africans and Asians demonstrates that colonial peoples successfully borrowed key aspects of British culture without submitting to the demands of British imperialism.

Furthermore, the widespread popularity of British styles of dress and recreation also reflect the contradictory but potent influence of the popular culture of British imperialism. Most British missionaries and colonial officials affected upper-class styles of Victorian dress to establish their credentials as gentlemen, which established Western clothing as a symbol of affluence, education, and social status in most African and Asian societies. Mission converts, clerks, translators, and compradors therefore dressed as British gentlemen and played cricket, tennis, and croquet to demand political rights and social deference. By establishing their credentials as "civilized" men, they sought to acquire political rights by breaking through the social and racial barriers that reinforced their subordinate status.

Conversely, lower-class and uneducated colonial peoples who did not embrace British culture also used Western-style clothing, but to subvert the imperial order. In the early decades of the twentieth century, a form of popular dance known as Beni spread throughout East Africa. Beni consisted of competing troupes of dancers who satirized European popular culture and military brass bands by affecting elaborate and often outrageous Western styles of dress. African soldiers in Nyasaland sang *"Amekwiba sokosi ya Bwana Major"* (he has stolen the major's socks) during their celebrations, which led some officials to worry seriously that Beni might undermine military discipline and destabilize colonial society. Their fears that dancing societies might inspire Africans to turn to burglary to acquire European clothing never materialized, and Beni was a matter of entertainment rather than politics. Moreover, the tangible rewards that came with the assimilation of British culture limited the appeal of these movements and ultimately accelerated the spread of British values and institutions throughout the empire.

INDIAN INFLUENCES ON THE EMPIRE

Although historians have written extensively about the cultural impact of British imperialism on non-Western peoples, not enough attention has been paid to the influence of Africans and Asians on the culture of the empire. British values and customs helped restructure colonial societies, but subject populations often modified them to contest the authority and legitimacy of the imperial system. By adapting British institutions to suit local circumstances, Africans and Asians fundamentally altered the cultural cornerstones of British rule. Furthermore, the very nature of indirect rule and informal influence required British imperialists to co-opt and assimilate non-Western cultures. Therefore British imperialism did not simply transfer British culture to the far corners of the globe; Britain's formal rule and informal influence established interlocking networks of exchange that created a hybrid multiethnic culture for the empire.

The "Indian" nature of the empire provides an especially interesting example of this process. As one of the oldest, largest, and most valuable British colonial territories, India exerted a profound influence on the greater British Empire. Colonial officials perfected indirect rule in India, and both the British East India Company and the Raj became training grounds for administrators before they were posted to other territories. As a result, British officials often applied Indian solutions to problems in Africa and other parts of Asia. In 1869, the chief commissioner for India's central provinces even traveled to Great Britain itself to assist local officials in adapting the Bengal Tenancy Act to Ireland. Moreover, Indians themselves moved freely within the empire as merchants, soldiers, and indentured laborers. Although the ruling culture of the empire was predominantly British, in most territories Indian customs and traditions had an equal (if not greater) influence on the everyday flow of imperial life.

British officials and their Indian allies were the primary agents of this cultural diffusion. Most of the British consuls who ran the Chinese treaty ports in the mid-nineteenth century were posted from India, and the police force of Shanghai's international settlement was largely composed of Sikhs. Similarly, many senior British civil servants in South Africa, including Lord Macartney and Sir John Craddock, began their careers in India. This Indian connection intensified after the partition of the continent when men like Frederick Lugard (later Lord Lugard) adapted the system of indirect rule to Africa. Lugard, who began his career as an officer in the Indian army, won Buganda for Britain as an employee of the British East Africa Company and eventually became the governor of Nigeria.

On the military side, Indian sepoys fought for Britain in China, Persia (1856), Egypt (1882), Burma (1885), Nyasaland (1893), and Uganda (1896). Moreover, British officers and Indian noncommissioned officers on secondment from the Indian army were the military experts of the empire. Before moving into colonial administration, Frederick Lugard organized Britain's colonial armies in both East and West Africa. As a result, Lugard and his contemporaries popularized Indian military traditions in British Africa and Asia, particularly the belief that only "martial races" could be recruited as soldiers. These stereotypes tended to fix ethnic identity throughout the empire, and they contributed to the growth of "tribalism" in Africa.

India's administrative, military, and cultural institutions also shaped the popular culture of the empire. The rupee became the standard currency for British colonial territories throughout Asia and East Africa. In the latter case, the East Africa Protectorate also adopted Indian civil and penal codes, and most of the new urban centers in the region were built around a central business district modeled on the Indian bazaar. Similarly, Lachlan Macquarie, the governor of New South Wales in the early nineteenth century and a career Indian army officer, introduced the Indian bungalow's verandah to Australian architecture; many of the buildings in the Chinese treaty ports followed Anglo-Indian styles, with squared columns and their own sweeping verandahs. Thus the British Empire gradually took on an Indian appearance as the imperial century progressed.

Although Christianity provided the ideological underpinning of British imperialism, Prime Minister Benjamin Disraeli often depicted Britain as a great Muslim power to discourage the Russians from exploiting anticolonial sentiment in India. With the postmutiny Indian army composed primarily of Muslims and Sikhs, the British military establishment became convinced that Muslims made the bravest and most reliable soldiers. British officers took these biases with them to East Africa, where Christian missionaries complained that the colonial army turned African soldiers into Muslims. Hinduism does not have a strong evangelical orientation, but Islam spread to almost every British colony in which there was a strong Indian influence.

Yet the "Indianization" of the empire in the nineteenth century was due to more than just the dissemination of Indian culture. As Britain's imperial influence expanded around the globe, large numbers of Indians emigrated, often under duress, to other British colonies. Merchants and sepoys made up a small part of this dispersal, but most Indians left the subcontinent as indentured laborers. Over the course of the imperial century approximately 5 million Indians went to work on Ceylonese tea estates, Malayan rubber plantations, Burmese rice farms, the Uganda railway, and sugar plantations in Fiji, Mauritius, Natal, and the Caribbean. British imperialists also relied on large numbers of indentured Chinese servants for agricultural work in Malaya and Australia and mine labor in South Africa. Taken as a whole, Chinese and Indian emigration in the nineteenth century must be counted along with the African slave trade and the European settlement of North America as one of the great population shifts of world history.

The British government's formal abolition of slavery throughout the empire in 1834 set this process in motion. As the growing middle class in Europe and North America developed an appetite for candy, baked goods, and sweetened tea, British sugar growers faced a chronic shortage of disciplined and affordable labor. After their attempts to force former slaves to continue working as apprentices failed, and European indentured servants from Britain proved too vulnerable to tropical diseases, sugar planters looked to India for relief. Colonial governments in South Africa and in Britain's West Indian sugar-producing colonies sympathized with this problem and subsidized the recruitment of non-European workers in India and in the Chinese treaty ports.

Many Indians were duped into signing contracts by unscrupulous recruiters who concealed the true terms of indentured service, but others became labor migrants voluntarily to escape difficult conditions in India. Pushed by population pressure, poverty, rising rents and taxes, famine, and the decline of Indian handicraft industries, they chose to seek their fortunes abroad. In doing so they suffered terribly on the densely packed ships that carried them to the far corners of the empire. At midcentury, mortality rates reached almost 20 percent on the longer voyages to the Caribbean.

Under the terms of the most common contracts, Indians agreed to work overseas for five years in return for regular wages and a return ticket to India upon completion of their term. Indentured servants worked for low wages, but their primary value lay in their contractual obligation not to change employers in search of better pay and working conditions. Without any legal means of contesting unfair labor practices, the indentured worker's lot was particularly hard. Plantation owners often used corporal punishment to discipline employees who demanded better terms, and they could count on sympathetic colonial courts to prosecute indentured servants who broke their contracts by running away. British officials in India tried to ensure that Indians received fair treatment while overseas and temporarily suspended recruiting operations altogether when conditions grew particularly bad. But they did not have the influence in London to thwart the politically powerful sugar growers. It took mounting criticism from Indian nationalists during the First World War to finally put an end to foreign labor recruiting in India.

The legacy of these dramatic population shifts was profound. Although most indentured servants expected only a brief sojourn abroad, many eventually took up permanent residence in Africa, Fiji, and the Caribbean because they lacked either the funds or the inclination to return home. Only a quarter of the approximately 340,000 Indians who emigrated to the Indian Ocean island of Mauritius between 1842 and 1900 ever returned to India. Other repatriation rates ranged from as high as 90 percent in Burma to as low as 20 percent in Trinidad, where the colonial government sought to solve its labor shortage by offering free land to indentured servants.

Most British administrators, however, worried that Indians would clash with indigenous populations or compete with European settler communities. They therefore used high taxes and trade licensing fees to discourage indentured servants from becoming permanent residents. The governor of the East Africa Protectorate refused to grant Indian workers land along the Uganda railway on the grounds that the colony was reserved for European settlement. Similarly, South African officials feared that former laborers who moved into commerce would take business away from European merchants and imposed an annual tax of £3 on every Indian resident to force them out of the territory.

Nevertheless, these discriminatory tactics did not prevent former indentured laborers from founding Indian communities throughout the Caribbean, the Pacific, and Anglophone Africa. These expatriate enclaves became self-sustaining rather quickly because British officials tried to prevent Indian workers from fighting over women by insisting that approximately one-third of all labor migrants had to be female. As a result, Indians replaced former African slaves as the dominant population group on Reunion, Mauritius, and many sugar-growing islands in the West Indies. On Trinidad and the Pacific island of Fiji they constituted approximately 30 percent of the total population. In South Africa, Indians outnumbered Europeans in Natal by the end of the nineteenth century. These transplanted Indian communities were products of the labor demands of British imperialism but contributed to the "Indianization" of the empire by spreading the language, customs, and material culture of India around the world.

IMPERIAL INFLUENCES ON BRITAIN

It would be an exaggeration to argue that British imperialism's dispersion of non-Western peoples and their customs had the same cultural impact on metropolitan Britain that it had on the rest of the empire. Only a tiny handful of Britain's colonial subjects ever visited the imperial metropole, and even fewer actually settled there. Moreover, the British population was so confident in its technological and moral superiority that few Britons were ever seriously tempted to adopt the cultural institutions of the colonies. Nevertheless, the acquisition of a global empire transformed British society in a number of direct and subtle ways. As noted in previous chapters, a broad spectrum of financiers, industrialists, merchants, bureaucrats, and members of the gentry profited directly from the expansion of British imperialism. On a less tangible level, the empire's non-Western customs and traditions markedly influenced the popular culture of Britain itself over the course of the imperial century.

British politicians and intellectuals were aware of at least some aspects of this process and worried about the contaminating influences of the empire on British society. In the eighteenth century, high-ranking employees of the British East India Company amassed huge personal fortunes by winning the privilege of collecting Bengal land revenues for the Mughal emperor. Many of these nabobs, as they were commonly known, used their wealth to buy large estates and acquire seats in the House of Commons after returning to Britain. The British gentry distrusted the foreign origins of these "new men," and in 1787 Edmund Burke personally prosecuted Warren Hastings, the chief architect of British India, on the charge of misusing Bengal land revenues and extorting funds from Indian rulers. Burke argued that constitutional rule in Britain had to be protected from men like Hastings who had become, in effect, a despotic Asian potentate. Similarly, evangelical reformers and abolitionists condemned the willingness of Company officials to tolerate "immoral" Indian practices under the system of indirect rule and worried that the corrupting influences of the empire might somehow spread to Britain.

Although this small but vocal coalition of middle-class reformers and humanitarians never stepped back from their criticism of imperialism, many British politicians developed a greater appreciation of the empire over the course of the imperial century. As population growth, rapid industrialization, and the threat of radical socialism sparked fears of widespread popular unrest, Disraeli and his Tory successors sought to preserve social stability by celebrating Britain's imperial genius. In depicting the empire as a symbol of Britain's heroism and national superiority, they played down ethnic and class differences in British society, in addition to courting lower-class voters in national elections. As noted in chapter 1, most British Liberals were equally committed to imperial causes and, for the most part, only differed with Conservatives on how the empire should be governed.

Interestingly enough, the legal restrictions banning Africans and Asians from participating in the political process in the colonies did not apply to Britain itself. In the 1890s, a pair of Indian expatriates living in Britain were actually elected to the House of Commons. Dadabhai Naoroji became the representative for Central Finsbury in 1892, and three years later Sir M. M. Bhownagree captured the seat for Green North-East. Bhownagree won by calling for greater economic centralization in the empire, but Naoroji rode to victory on the public backlash against Lord Salisbury's statement that British voters would never elect a black man. Clearly the colonies were not simply reflections or extensions of British society, and metropolitan politicians could not mobilize support for their domestic or foreign policies simply by invoking Britain's imperial greatness.

Although it is difficult to determine how much British voters were swayed by imperialist political rhetoric, imperial issues ranging from the search for David Livingstone to the purchase of the Suez Canal shares to the Anglo-Boer War captured the British public's popular imagination during the final decades of the nineteenth century. London music halls offered nationalistic performances celebrating the glory and unity of the empire. The newly literate middle and lower classes avidly consumed magazines and newspapers that presented a similarly romanticized view of imperial issues. Colonial correspondents turned Britain's countless small colonial wars into great heroic adventures, depicting the fall of Khartoum and the death of Gordon as a morality play about a devout Christian's lone struggle against great hordes of slave-trading heathen.

Similarly, Rudyard Kipling (best known for *The Jungle Book*), Rider Haggard (the author of *King Solomon's Mines*), and other popular imperial writers captured the reading public's attention with fictionalized accounts of British adventurers in exotic African and Asian settings. These authors invariably demonized non-Western leaders who fought to retain their sovereignty and romanticized Britain's imperial expansion. Contemporary history textbooks stressed similar themes in the schools by emphasizing the morality and courage of the empire's founders. By devouring these heroic tales, future colonial officials learned the moral certainty and cultural self-confidence they would need to govern their non-Western subjects.

Yet the celebration of the empire had a number of subtle and unforeseen influences on metropolitan British society. Non-Western styles of dress and decoration filtered into common use through the general public's growing romantic infatuation with exotic non-Western cultures. Imperial exhibitions drew large crowds to displays of stuffed tropical animals and models of "native villages" in artificial jungles, and the middle classes emulated aristocratic colonial elites by decorating their homes with stuffed animal heads and similar imperial totems. Tea, sugar, cocoa, and other agricultural products of the empire became staple foods in most households, and low-cost tropical oils helped create new standards of personal hygiene by making soap more affordable.

India had the greatest influence on metropolitan British society of all non-Western colonial territories by virtue of its importance and long-term contact with Britain. In 1928, the *Oxford English Dictionary* listed approximately nine hundred English words that had Indian origins. Some of the more common examples still in use today include shampoo, khaki, pajamas, polo, buggy, pundit, jungle, loot (from *lootie,* a band of plundering thieves), and thug (from *thagi,* a religious sect that preyed on travelers). Many English terms for clothing and textiles also have Indian origins: calico, chintz, dungaree, bandanna, seersucker, and cashmere. British officials in India had to learn new words to understand Indian society, and these new terms inevitably found their way into everyday English as connections between India and Britain intensified over the course of the imperial century.

Although British customs and institutions were useful instruments of social control in the colonies, metropolitan British society was also profoundly influenced by the process of becoming a global imperial power. British imperialists may have denigrated non-Western cultures to rationalize depriving subject peoples of their sovereignty, but they also had to assimilate African and Asian values and traditions to make the imperial system work. Moreover, the partisans of empire also romanticized these non-Western cultures to convince the British public to support the imperial enterprise. In doing so they introduced significant African and Asian elements into British popular culture, thereby refuting the assumption that the empire had little influence on the historical development of metropolitan Britain.

BRITISH IMPERIALISM AND THE PROCESS OF
ENVIRONMENTAL AND BIOLOGICAL CHANGE

Thus far this book has focused primarily on processes of cross-cultural exchange driven by Britain's imperial expansion in the nineteenth century. Yet in addition to facilitating the movement of peoples and cultures throughout the empire, British imperialism also dispersed plants, animals, and microbes around the globe. In doing so, British imperialists accelerated the ongoing process of globalization that intensified in the sixteenth century as a result of the maritime revolution and Columbian voyages. British scientists and settlers often intentionally transferred useful plants and animals throughout the empire to achieve specific economic ends. Conversely, they also brought about unforeseen environmental and epidemiological changes simply by reconfiguring political boundaries and linking previously isolated regions of the world into an increasingly integrated series of overlapping economic systems. As has already been noted, the introduction of Old World diseases to Australia and North America proved fatal to most of their indigenous populations.

British botanists played a primary role in this process of biological diffusion. By identifying and propagating economically useful plants, they developed commercial applications of imperialism. Kew Gardens, originally a London royal residence, became Britain's main botanical clearinghouse and research center by the mid-nineteenth century. Researchers at Kew oversaw and coordinated a network of subsidiary botanical gardens throughout the empire that introduced tea, cinnamon, and tobacco to India, transferred rubber trees from Brazil to Ceylon, and laid the groundwork for a nascent timber industry in Central Africa. After collecting over a million new specimens by the beginning of the twentieth century, imperial botanists shifted their efforts to developing the commercial applications of known plants. Working in tandem with the Imperial Institute's Scientific and Technical Research Department, their main goal was to enhance the profitability of the empire.

Yet these imperial biological exchanges also served a strategic function. In the 1850s British botanists traveled secretly to South America to collect samples of the Cinchona tree, the only naturally occurring source of quinine. Since daily doses of quinine were the only effective protection against malaria, Britain's imperial expansion in the tropics depended on a reliable and steady supply of the drug. Therefore British botanists established Cinchona plantations in the Indian highlands to provide inexpensive low-grade quinine for the armed forces.

The exchange of biological material increased the security and profitability of the empire but came at an extremely high cost. The exotic plants that imperial botanists introduced into African and Asian ecosystems often pushed out native species. More significantly, British imperialism accelerated the diffusion of disease-causing microbes around the globe, thereby sparking virulent epidemics among previously isolated populations that lacked defenses to the new pathogens. With the Amerindian and Aboriginal populations of North America and Australia largely wiped out, Africans and Asians now faced the biological consequences of Britain's global empire.

Cholera was an endemic Indian disease that had previously been limited to the subcontinent by virtue of its extremely short incubation period. In the mid-nineteenth century, British imperialism helped touch off a series of global cholera pandemics after steamships reduced travel times to India. The disease killed millions of people throughout Africa, the Middle East, Europe, and the Americas by spreading along Britain's network of imperial communications and the pilgrimage routes to Mecca. Similarly, an outbreak of the bubonic plague in Hong Kong in 1894 quickly reached Asia and Africa by the turn of the century. In India, where the disease was virtually unknown before the 1890s, it spread to virtually every province within a few short years. Over half a million people died in the Punjab alone, causing a 3 percent drop in the region's total population.

Thus historians of Africa have described the thirty years between partition and the First World War as the most deadly decades in the history of the continent. Although malaria and other tropical fevers were endemic to much of precolonial Africa, virulent epidemics were relatively rare. Large sections of the continent had little direct contact with the wider world, and in coastal regions peoples like the West African Asante developed a simple inoculation against smallpox that involved infecting a patient with a mild form of the disease through a series of skin punctures.

European imperialism upset this epidemiological balance by exposing vulnerable African populations to new pathogens. Military conquest and improved transportation eliminated geographical and political barriers, bringing previously isolated societies into direct contact with new infectious diseases. Similarly, by establishing game reserves, clearing forests, and introducing widespread irrigation, conservationists, settlers, and colonial officials created new breeding environments for mosquitoes and tsetse flies, which were the main vectors for malaria and trypanosomiasis (sleeping sickness). Moreover, the very presence of Europeans and their Arab and Indian clients also introduced smallpox, typhoid, cholera, and measles into the most vulnerable African societies of the hinterland. As was pointed out in chapter 3, these environmental changes produced widespread epidemics throughout eastern and southern Africa just when Africans were struggling to resist the European partition of the continent.

Moreover, most African societies were further weakened by Britain's unintentional introduction of equally virulent infectious cattle diseases to the continent. In 1853 British settlers imported a number of Friesian bulls into South Africa that carried lung sickness. The disease spread quickly to African herds at a time when many societies in Natal and the eastern Cape were under pressure from the Afrikaners and British settlers. This incident was only a precursor of the much more devastating bovine pneumonia epidemic that ravaged Africa in the 1890s. Known as rinderpest, this highly contagious disease caused severe fever, violent diarrhea, and mouth blisters before the animal eventually died of dehydration and starvation in just six to twelve days.

The infected cattle and oxen that were the most likely source of the rinderpest came from India, introduced into northeast Africa in the late 1880s by either British forces in the Sudan or the Italian army in Ethiopia. The disease was so virulent that it spread as fast as twenty miles per day by infecting wild game and domestic herds of cattle. It reached the Cape Colony in southern Africa by 1897. Sheep and goats remained unaffected, but African pastoralists and European ranchers lost up to 90 percent of their herds. In South Africa alone, the epidemic destroyed over one-third of all the cattle in the Transvaal and Orange Free State.

Although these bovine epidemics created considerable problems for European settlers, they were absolutely catastrophic for African pastoral and semipastoral peoples in eastern and southern Africa. Since livestock was a measure of wealth in many African societies, rinderpest left most cattle herders dangerously vulnerable to famine and also wiped out their savings. The resulting upheaval weakened African institutions of political authority, thereby contributing to the social divisions that made British imperialism possible. Moreover, rinderpest accelerated the colonial transformation of Africans into subordinate wage laborers by forcing them to look for paid employment to purchase food and restock their herds.

British imperialists were only dimly aware of the ecological and epidemiological consequences of their actions. Although European doctors developed a much greater understanding of the causes of infectious disease over the course of the imperial century, most officials, settlers, missionaries, and merchants considered epidemics and famine a natural part of life in the tropics. Lacking the means and the inclination to solve these problems, they instead sought to isolate themselves from the subject population, which they considered the ultimate source of most diseases.

As the empire expanded, many Britons developed a powerful fear of the tropics that was based on both medical reality and pure superstition. In eighteenth-century India, the British East India Company lost up to 75 percent of its new employees during their first year in the country. Even in the nineteenth century, British troops in India still suffered mortality rates of almost 7 percent per year, over four times the death rate of their comrades stationed in Britain.

In the absence of reliable medical information on the causes of infectious disease, British imperialists attributed these high mortality rates to a variety of pseudoscientific causes. In the late nineteenth century, Western doctors blamed many tropical ailments on "actinic radiation." Led by U.S. neurologists, they concluded that dark-skinned peoples had a natural defense against the photochemical effects of the ultraviolet band of the spectrum. Conversely, they believed that intense sunlight in Africa and Asia damaged the nerve tissues of Caucasians, thereby causing insomnia, memory loss, lethargy, and insanity. Tropical doctors used terms like "tropical amnesia" and "Punjab head" to explain the fatigue, diarrhea, headaches, ulcers, sexual problems, alcoholism, and suicides they diagnosed in their British patients. They also developed a series of outlandish and comical preventative devices to guard against tropical diseases. Some of the more noteworthy quacks and self-appointed medical experts recommended a flannel "cholera belt" to ward off unhealthy chills in the evening and a solar topi to protect the head and neck from unhealthy sunlight. Many "imperial ailments" were due to organic causes, but others were most likely brought on by the stress and insecurity that came from being a privileged minority in an alien colonial society.

In practice, however, serious public health in the British Empire was based largely on the principle of physical and social segregation between Europeans and the non-Western population. Most foreign settlements in colonial cities were surrounded by a greenbelt consisting of carefully manicured parks and golf courses to insulate European families from the contaminating influence of Africans and Asians. Urban planners in Sierra Leone even calculated the nightly flight radius of a mosquito so they could locate Freetown's European suburbs a "safe" distance from African neighborhoods. Needless to say, these privileged suburbs were also the only areas equipped with running water and modern sewers.

British officials did not have the resources or the inclination to extend comprehensive medical care and basic urban services to non-Western neighborhoods. Yet colonial administrators were ever mindful that widespread disease and famine could lead to economic disruption, social turmoil, and even political unrest. They therefore responded to the threat of contagious disease by subjecting key segments of the colonial population to forced segregation and mandatory medical treatment. Infected domestic servants and prostitutes threatened their European clients, and the British Empire relied on healthy colonial soldiers and laborers for its security and economic vitality.

British medical officials were more concerned with utility and efficiency than with respecting the interests or sensibilities of non-Western patients. As "protected persons" rather than citizens, Africans and Asians had little say in the formulation of colonial public health policy. In India, the Epidemic Disease Act of 1888 empowered the government to detain and treat suspected carriers of the plague without regard to their status, faith, or gender. Devout Hindus complained that the quarantine measures violated caste laws and considered the forced inspection of women a form of sexual molestation. Public health officials also used the act to restrict long-distance travel and destroy any Indian home or business found to be harboring the infected rats that spread the plague. Similarly, British officials in southern Africa tried to contain rinderpest outbreaks through the wholesale slaughter of African-owned cattle.

These draconian measures achieved a measure of success in limiting the spread of infectious disease, but they also intensified African and Asian opposition to the most inequitable aspects of British imperialism.

With considerable justification, Britain's subjects suspected that colonial public health measures were also intended to assist in reordering non-Western economies and societies to serve British interests. The London Missionary Society saw rinderpest as an opportunity to teach Africans the virtues of paid employment, and the South African Chamber of Mines exploited the resulting labor surplus to increase working hours while cutting African wages by 30 percent. In India, British officials used the plague as an excuse to undermine the authority of elected Indian city councils on the grounds that they had not taken the necessary steps to contain the epidemic.

In many cases these public health measures were so invasive that they brought about the very unrest they were designed to contain. In Basutoland (modern Lesotho), widespread rumors accused Europeans of intentionally spreading the rinderpest, and the unpopular measures used to control the cattle epidemic led to an armed uprising that laid the groundwork for African political opposition to imperialism. Similarly, Indians opposed the public health policies of the Raj by spreading rumors that Britain invented the plague to create work for European doctors, steal Indian property, and conceal news of an alleged anti-British uprising in the countryside. In 1897 dissatisfaction with the Epidemic Disease Act grew so intense that the British plague commissioner for the city of Pune was assassinated by outraged Indians who would no longer tolerate the government's unprecedented intervention in their daily lives.

The consequences of the environmental aspects of Britain's imperial system were decidedly mixed. British imperialists created economic opportunities for themselves and their colonial subjects by introducing useful plants and animals into their overseas possessions. The severe ecological and epidemiological upheavals produced by this process facilitated British imperial expansion by undermining political authority and the established social order in non-Western societies. Moreover, colonial public health policies reinforced the subordinate status of Africans and Asians in colonial society and helped transform them into disciplined wage laborers. Yet the environmental and biological changes introduced by British imperialism also made colonial rule more precarious by provoking unrest. In many cases African and Asian dissatisfaction with invasive conservation and public health measures helped organize political resistance to the imperial system.

In conclusion, it is clear that the expansion of British imperialism in the nineteenth century can best be understood as the creation of a global network of unequal exchanges. Through the mechanisms of free trade, informal influence, and formal rule, British imperialists diffused people, capital, commodities, languages, cultures, plants, animals, and microbes around the globe. The imperial system did not simply transfer British authority and institutions to the colonies while extracting wealth in return. There can be no question that the imperial balance sheet was vastly weighted in Britain's favor and that many Africans and Asians suffered tremendously from the loss of their sovereignty. Nevertheless, British imperialism was only viable when it won sufficient allies among the subject population. Britain needed cooperative compradors, dragomans, commercial brokers, and mission converts to exploit political, ethnic, religious, and class divisions in African and Asian societies. Without these non-Western confederates the British would have had to rely on military force alone to build their overseas empire.

In reality, Britain's imperial system was extremely fragile. Although British imperialists enjoyed a considerable advantage in wealth and technology over most non-Western societies in the nineteenth century, they lacked the political resolve, military reserves, financial resources, and administrative manpower to simply impose their will on the colonial majority. As a privileged but isolated minority in colonial society, British merchants, missionaries, settlers, and administrators developed the institution of indirect rule to compensate for their weaknesses. By co-opting and adapting the values and customs of their colonial subjects, they reduced the cost of the imperial enterprise by strengthening their authority and legitimacy in the eyes of the general population.

As a result, indirect rule forced British officials to entice a segment of African and Asian society to participate in the imperial enterprise. Britain's need to understand and assimilate indigenous cultural institutions, coupled with the threat of widespread unrest, allowed the colonial majority to influence imperial policy. The Indian Mutiny of 1857 taught British imperialists that it was dangerous to ignore the values and ambitions of their non-Western subjects. Africans and Asians who successfully depicted themselves as the arbiters of "tradition" could exploit the weakness and ignorance of British administrators to achieve a measure of social and economic mobility. They used the values and institutions of their British rulers to challenge the most invasive aspects of the imperial system, and Britain's African and Asian subjects as a whole exerted a strong influence on the popular culture of the empire by virtue of their importance and numbers. Moreover, the legacy of the cultural and biological exchanges resulting from British imperialism were part of the broader process of globalization that continues to this day.

SUGGESTIONS FOR FURTHER READING

Bailey, Richard. *Images of English: A Cultural History of the Language*. Ann Arbor: University of Michigan Press, 1991.

Brantlinger, Patrick. *Rule of Darkness: British Literature and Imperialism, 1830–1914*. Ithaca, N.Y.: Cornell University Press, 1988.

Headrick, Daniel. *The Tentacles of Progress: Technology Transfer in the Age of Imperialism, 1850–1940*. New York: Oxford University Press, 1988.

MacKenzie, John, ed. *Imperialism and the Natural World*. Manchester: Manchester University Press, 1990.

————. *Imperialism and Popular Culture*. Manchester: Manchester University Press, 1992.

Mangan, J. A., ed. *The Imperial Curriculum: Racial Images and Education in the British Colonial Experience*. New York: Routledge, 1993.

Northrup, David. *Indentured Labor in the Age of Imperialism*. Cambridge: Cambridge University Press, 1995.

Patterson, G., and K. D. Hartwig, eds. *Disease in African History*. Durham, N.C.: Duke University Press, 1978.

Rao, G. Subba. *Indian Words in English: A Study in Indo-British Cultural and Linguistic Relations*. Oxford: Clarendon, 1969.

Walls, Andrew. *The Missionary Movement in Christian History: Studies in the Transmission of Faith*. Maryknoll, N.Y.: Orbis, 1996.

INDEX

Abdulhamid, 110, 114, 115
Aborigines, 4, 13, 123–124
Adderley, Sir Charles, 16, 21, 67
Aden, 5, 18
Afrikaners, 60–61, 76–79, 82–83. *See
also* South Africa
Afro-Victorians, 67–69, 82, 87–88,
131
Amerindians, 4, 123–124
Argentina, 18, 19, 123
Asante Confederation, 66–67, 73, 87,
141
Australia, 13, 15, 123–124
Awadh, 35, 47

Baker, Samuel, 64
Baluchistan, 5
Basutoland (Lesotho), 26, 145
Bechuanaland (Lesotho), 26
British East India Company, 4, 10, 29,
31, 35; abolition of, 47–48; con-
quest of India, 35; influence on
Britain, 137; mortality rates of em-
ployees, 143; political role, 38;
trade with China, 96–97
Beni, 132
Berlin Conference of 1884–1885, 71
Bhownagree, Sir M.M., 138
British Levant Company, 108
British South Africa Company, 78, 85

Brussels Treaty of 1890, 72
Burke, Edmund, 137
Burma, 5, 26
Burton, Richard, 64
Buxton, Thomas Fowell, 11, 20, 62

Canada, 12–13, 15
Canning, Lord, 49
Canning, Stratford, 108
Cape Colony, 15, 61, 76, 79, 83
Chamberlain, Joseph, 23, 84, 103
China, 18, 19, 27, 31; Boxer Rebel-
lion, 104–105; British trade with,
100–101; Canton System, 93, 97,
98; Ch'ing Dynasty, 93, 95, 101,
105; compradors, 100; European
spheres of influence in, 102–103;
self-strengthening, 103–104; Tai-
ping Rebellion, 101; treaty ports,
99–100, 133
Clive, Robert, 36
Cobden, Richard, 11, 16
Corn Laws, 11
Crimean War, 110–111
Cyprus, 111

Disraeli, Benjamin, 23, 47, 48, 112,
134, 137

Egypt, 26, 29, 69, 70, 95; British administration of, 114; British occu-

pation of, 113–114; debt, 12. *See also* Muhammad Ali

Ethiopia, 18

Evangelical Protestants. *See* missions

Falkland Islands, 5, 18

France, 36, 72, 102, 113, 114

Gambia, 12, 60, 66

Great Britain: army, 22; colonial administration, 27, 29, 133; electoral reform, 23; emigration from, 12–13, 82, 122–123; industry, 10, 21; influence of empire, 137–139; investment, 24, 70; trade, 11, 16, 23

gentlemanly capitalists, 24

Germany, 73, 78–79, 102, 116

Gladstone, William, 23, 113, 114

Gold Coast (Ghana), 12, 66, 84

Goldie, Sir George, 72–73, 81

Gordon, Sir Charles, 101, 114, 138

Great Depression of 1873, 22, 23, 69

Hastings, Warren, 137

Hobson, J.A., 78

Hong Kong, 5, 18, 27, 98, 99, 103

Horton, James Africanus, 69, 88

Hudson's Bay Company, 13

Hyam, Ronald, 1

Ibo, 87

indentured servitude, 134–136

Indian Mutiny, 22, 25, 45–48. *See also* India

Indian National Congress, 56–57

indirect rule, 30, 81, 89, 120, 129, 146

India: administration of, 35–36, 39–40, 44, 48–49, 55; agricultural reform, 37–38, 41–42, 52–53, 56; army, 38–39, 48, 51, 54, 133; Bengal, 35–36, 46, 47; British invest-

ment in, 50–51, 53; British trade with, 49–50, 53; civil service, 48, 56; cultural influences of, 133–134; education, 43–44; railways, 50, 52, 55; revenues, 37–38, 40–41, 49, 51, 97; Utilitarians, 43, 47, 48. *See also* Mughal Empire; Princely States

ivory, 63, 65

Janissaries, 94, 95, 107. *See also* Ottoman Empire

Japan, 102

Kenya (East Africa Protectorate), 26, 73–75, 81–82, 134; native reserves, 86; settlers, 75, 82, 84–85

Khan, Sir Sayyid Ahmed, 57

legitimate commerce, 62–64

Lin Tse-hsu, 98

Livingstone, David, 63–65, 138

Lugard, Lord, 30, 74, 133

Maasai, 75–76

Macaulay, Thomas, 43

MacKinnon, Sir William, 73–75, 81

Mahmud II, 107

malaria, 12, 25, 140–141, 142

Malaya, 26

Manchester School, 16

Maori, 14, 15, 124–125

Mauritius, 11, 136

mercantilism, 10, 38

Midhat Pasha, 107

missions, 20, 128–129; Africa, 68, 74, 88, 130–131, 145; China, 97, 100, 101, 116–117; India, 42–43, 129–130; Protestant Evangelicals, 19–21, 42, 66, 72

Mughal Empire, 31, 34–35, 39, 48

Muhammad Ali, 95, 107, 109

Mungo Park, 60, 64, 65

ABOUT THE AUTHOR

TIMOTHY PARSONS holds a joint appointment in the History Department and the African and Afro-American Studies Program as an assistant professor at Washington University in St. Louis. Specializing in the social history of colonial Africa and the British Empire, he has conducted field research on both African military service and colonial education in Kenya, Malawi, and South Africa. Dr. Parsons is also the author of *The African Rank-and-File: Social Implications of Colonial Service in the King's African Rifles, 1902–1964* (forthcoming from the Heinemann Social History of Africa series) and several journal articles on African social history.